SOME PEOPLE AREN'T MEANT TO BE SAVED

SOME PEOPLE AREN'T MEANT TO BE SAVED

Summer Kaur

Some People Aren't Meant to be Saved Copyright © 2021 by Summer Kaur

All rights reserved. No part of this publication may be reproduced, stored in a retrieval system, or transmitted, in any form, or by any means (electronic, mechanical, photocopying, recording or otherwise) without the prior written permission of the publisher.

This novel is a work of fiction. Names, characters, places and incidents either are products of the author's imagination or are used factiously.

Author Name
Summer Kaur

ISBN 979-8-5328-6453-5
Independently published

First printed: July 2021

TABLE OF CONTENTS

GETTING AWAY	2
THE FIRST BIT	21
CHANGE	42
ONE STEP AT A TIME	60
THE THINGS YOU CAN'T CHANGE	75
NASTY SURPRISES	94
DRUNK THERAPY	105
DIFFICULT TRUTHS	123
KNOWING WHEN TO WALK AWAY	134
A HARSH REALITY	146
BEFORE IT'S TOO LATE	162
THE END OF THE ROAD	174
LIFE AFTER	190
AUTHOR BIO	203

SOME PEOPLE AREN'T MEANT TO BE SAVED

SOME PEOPLE AREN'T MEANT TO BE SAVED

GETTING AWAY

There's so much you won't grasp from the story that you are about to read. How do you fit years of abuse into one, short version of events?
I'm still not sure if abuse is even the right word to explain my situation, but somewhere along the line things stopped making sense, I know that for sure.
We grow up with a sketched idea of what is right and what is wrong but, where do you draw the line? Should there be a line? Is there a limit beyond the line where bad transcends to beyond repair? Broken and unfixable? How do you know when to give up is what I think I'm trying to ask? I make a few other insinuations there too which you'll probably have caught onto if you reflect as much as me. I'm sick of asking for a friend. I'm asking for myself and probably many others too. I'm tired of searching for the point. Services available, might as well not be.

SOME PEOPLE AREN'T MEANT TO BE SAVED

Some days I'm adamant I'm the problem. Certain.
'Some people don't want to be saved...' The last thing my sister said to me four years ago. I wish she hadn't given up on me. Sometimes it gets hard, especially the older Ellie gets. She's five now.
If standing by Ed made me guilty of anything, I guess it was only of love and if people struggle to understand that, then maybe I'm better off fixing this on my own. I'm used to it.
He loves me deep down; he always apologizes for the god-awful times. Okay yes ultimately, it's me that gets the brunt of the bad times, the shouting, the screaming, the...
But it's what you do right? You stand by them. Or at least that's what you vow to do. It's been tradition for longer than I care to be educated on, but it must mean something.
What sort of woman would I be, or mother even, if I were to give up on him? Ellie adores her dad.
In the same breath, I find myself battling with my own thoughts sometimes too. Don't get me wrong there have been times I have thought about leaving, but something always gets the better of me. I can't explain what that something is. I understand it in my head but, for some reason, whenever I try to explain it out loud it always sounds... excusing. He's struggled for a long time and I sympathise more than you'll know but my heart begs for answers all the time.
What did I do wrong? What do I do wrong? I have to play some part surely.
Then I jump to thoughts about times I've tried to help and show I care. Even when I used mum's inheritance to get him

SOME PEOPLE AREN'T MEANT TO BE SAVED

into rehab he fell straight off the bandwagon when he got out. He couldn't see why I was annoyed when he ungratefully reminded me, he hadn't asked me to do it! Even then, I'd be exaggerating the situation in his mind and being unsupportive in some way shape or form. I honestly can't win at the best of times.

The school, they pull me aside, ask me questions, judge my parenting - I can tell. If only they knew the half of it. I don't mind though. No one is as hard on me as I am, believe me.

'The father's a druggy' - whispers in the playground.

The only friend I did have to speak to is gone now her little boy is in high school. She drops a text at times, but we all have our own lives I suppose. Sometimes I just long that normal sense of connection, to have a conversation that isn't fueled by anger and malice.

Then again, I think I've forgotten how to talk to people normally so there probably wouldn't be a point anyway.

I was in an online mental health group until Ed found out about it and smashed my phone.

He gets paranoid.

I wasn't in there to gossip, I just wanted to feel understood, I guess.

He thought it would be a 'risky place' to try and 'make new friends' and that they would try and 'drag me down to their level'. Assumed they would try and convince me I wasn't happy in my home life.

How naive does he think I am? He makes me sound vulnerable.

Then it was 'I can't deal with you talking to strangers about our private lives', but I'm not like that.

But he insisted I had better things to do with my time than talk to a bunch of 'nosey bastards' about problems that were the norm for most relationships.

He doesn't know for obvious reasons, but I kept in touch with a guy from the group. We've never met. He initiated that we became pen-pals in the beginning. I thought it was weird at first, but we really gelled. He had this weird way of knowing what to say, I hadn't really had anybody understand my circumstances the way he did.

I know how it sounds. I know it might not make sense to others but it's not how it seems. For such a long time I felt alone and misunderstood.

It took me a while to open up.

Fear of being scrutinised, I guess.

Usually, people hear the stories and they'll be sympathetic for a while until they get sick of hearing them on repeat. Then comes the 'you need to leave him'... 'Honestly, I don't know what to say anymore if you want to keep putting up with it'.

I get it.

It's a shame they didn't get me.

I haven't heard from Pete for a few weeks so I'm beginning to worry a little. Although it's meant I haven't had to worry about Ed finding a letter in the post, or the 'long baths' I have to go and take just to write back undetected.

Ed's been in the worst mood today. We're skint. He's been pacing about everywhere, and Ellie's been getting under his feet.

SOME PEOPLE AREN'T MEANT TO BE SAVED

Usually, he does his best to hold himself together when Ellie's around but today was different.

He lost his job a few weeks ago - he was caught taking drugs on his lunch break.

So, the last month has been harder than usual, financially and atmospherically.

For the first time in a month, he raised his hand to me today. For the rest of the afternoon, I've sat upstairs with Ellie, getting crafty and trying to keep her out of Ed's way.

I heard the front door go downstairs.

"You could have posted this pal?", Ed said.

"One of them needed to be signed for so it's routine to knock, sorry if I disturbed you".

I recognised the voice... It was the postman. What could possibly need signing for?

Occasionally Pete's letter would need signing for, but it's been weeks now, I figured he'd found other things to be doing.

It's quiet downstairs. A million worries were passing through my mind and I couldn't help but get distracted from the crafts. I could hear Ellie in the background, 'what's wrong mummy?', 'mummy look, play', but I was lost for wonder - lost for worry.

Mind, if he found something, he shouldn't have by now he would have been up these stairs in a flash. I know Ed.

"Ellie, grab your teddy sweetheart, mummy needs a wee".

"Mummy you're a big girl now, you don't need me to come for a wee with you," said Ellie.

"WHAT THE FUCK IS THIS?", shouted Ed.

SOME PEOPLE AREN'T MEANT TO BE SAVED

"Ellie just grab your teddy and come with me!".
I picked her up and ran to the bathroom. As I shut the door, Ed was charging up the stairs, mouth gritted, eyes glaring.
"ALICE!".
I was struggling to lock the door, Ellie was crying, my heart beating ten to the dozen. Please just lock, please just lock. By this point he was outside the door, hand on the handle and finally it locked.
Ed was banging on the door.
I sat back against the door, Ellie in my lap, trying my best to cover her ears. I tried not to sob for her sake, but I found myself silently crying.
"OPEN THE DOOR AL!" he yelled as he kept knocking, getting more aggressive.
"I'm not just going to go away and neither will this, now open the goddamn door before I kick it in".
"I can't talk to you while you're in this mood Ed, it's not fair on Ellie!".
"Not fair on Ellie, NOT FAIR ON ELLIE - what you've done isn't fair ALICE".
"Mummy why is daddy angry?" whispered Ellie.
"Shhh," I said, as I stroked her head and kissed her forehead gently.
"Ed?" He didn't answer.
I gave it a couple of minutes then came out and walked Ellie into her room.
"Stay here baby, mummy will be back upstairs in a minute".
As I shut her door, I wiped my eyes and prepared for the worst.

SOME PEOPLE AREN'T MEANT TO BE SAVED

Walking down the stairs felt like a lifetime.
This is it.
Ed reacted shamefully when he found out I was in an online group, I just know he won't be as calm if he's found Pete's letter.
At this moment, I wondered if the last thing my sister said was in reference to me? Maybe it was me who didn't want to be saved?
I should have left a while ago.
I looked at the front door and genuinely contemplated running.
I didn't though. I felt almost programmed to walk into the front room.
Ed had a grasp of the letter with his head in his hands.
He stood up and threw the letter at me.
"You've done well to hide this from me, when did you plan on cracking the fucking news, Al?" he yelled as he waved the letter.
"Ed, I can explain..." but before I had time to finish, he interrupted me.
"How can you possibly explain that we might be losing our home Alice? Three months of arrears? Were you going to tell me when we were being escorted off the fucking premises? Or was it meant to be a fucking Father's Day surprise? You never fail to fuck up!"
Every ounce of me wanted to scream at him about his financial abuse for the drugs he liked to shove up his nose, but I think I was more relieved.
"I'm going to pick some stuff up, before I do something,

we'll both regret and when I'm back you better have figured an idea to sort this shit out".

I didn't speak back, for once I think I was just grateful to hear he was leaving the house. I needed to compose myself. It was a close call but one that made me second guess mine and Ellie's future in that split second. I'm fed up with treading on eggshells and taking care of all the serious shit. I keep my mouth shut and I'm exactly the way he expects me to be and for what?

As he left, I noticed the rest of the post on the side. There was a small package with it.

I checked the window to make sure he'd left then opened it. I was confused to see a little black notebook inside with a set of keys. I opened it up and there was a handwritten note in the front, from Pete.

It read,

'Hey Alice,

It's been a short while; I can only apologise. How have things been? How's little Ellie? I went for my consultation a couple of weeks ago to find out I only have a couple of weeks left. The cancer is far too aggressive this time.

Reading your last letter made me sad and even more so when I got my news. But that's not important. I thought you may appreciate this notebook. At present it's empty but I thought you could use it to keep writing to me. There's not much I can physically do to help from this point forward and I'm sorry we won't get to meet as arranged but my help doesn't end here. You're a special woman Alice and I hope that one day someone has the pleasure of letting you know this.

SOME PEOPLE AREN'T MEANT TO BE SAVED

All my love, Pete x'
I broke down.
Is that strange for a man I'd never met?
All my love? Something about that brought me warmth. Where was I going to hide this from Ed and what on earth were the keys for?
I went to hide it on top of the kitchen cupboard when a small piece of paper fell from the notebook. Bending down to pick it up, I noticed some writing on the back…
'Alice, take this and do what's best for you and Ellie. The keys? They're to my bungalow 10 miles out of town. This might be the end for me, but this could be a fresh start for the two of you. The money will help while you get settled and gather direction. Here's the address... The choice is yours. What you do is none of my business but at least you have the option now'.
On the reverse, was a cheque for £20,000!
I didn't even have to think. "Ellie, grab some of your favorite toys. I'm calling a taxi; we're going to see your aunty Lisa".
"YAY, okay mummy, two secs".
I knew Ed would be back soon, there was no time to pack. I'll get in touch in a day or two to finalise things. If Ed had found this instead of the notice letter, things could have been so different.
The taxi pulled up earlier than expected, I didn't even have time to gather anything, my head was a mess.
I was shaking.
I rushed Ellie out the door, but Ed was walking towards us. He looked more confused than anything. I bundled Ellie in

the taxi as fast I could, but he picked up pace and began running towards the taxi. He stopped looking confused the closer he got to the taxi.

"Please, help me" I cried out to the driver, "He's not going to let me go. Please".

I rushed into the taxi, but Ed was at the window.

He grabbed at the handle, but the driver locked the doors.

"UNLOCK THESE DOORS NOW" Ed shouted.

The driver tried to reason with him, but Ed was running low on patience.

"He's taken drugs, please just get us out of here" I begged the driver frantically.

"Don't worry, love, we're going" he replied.

BANG, BANG, BANG!

"Sir, please stop attacking the vehicle and stand aside, otherwise, I am going to have to alert authorities" the driver said to Ed.

He stepped away from the taxi, but he still looked angry.

"Alice, this isn't done with" Ed said, as the taxi drove off.

He watched us drive away.

I watched him too.

I was still in disbelief as I watched him screaming and shouting in the distance. I was lost in the fact that instead of being in the center of it, I was heading in the opposite direction.

I'm not quite sure how I was supposed to feel about that.

It didn't have the effect on me that I thought it would and my head just can't make sense of that. If this were right, it would feel right, wouldn't it? But I definitely don't feel as free as I

SOME PEOPLE AREN'T MEANT TO BE SAVED

thought I would.
"Mummy is Daddy coming to see aunty Lee later?"
All of a sudden, I felt awful.
We weren't going to see Lisa.
In fact, the more I tuned into reality and stopped thinking about myself, I realized I didn't actually know where we were going either.
I'm sitting in a car and heading to a destination I'm not quite sure of, with nothing but the clothes on my back, a couple of Ell's bits and a cheque I'm unsure will even cash.
All of a sudden, I felt irrational, sick and all those feelings you'd expect to come when making drastic life changes.
There I go again. Making it all about me.
Ed will probably think I'm doing this for attention. Either way, it will be driving him insane that he can't be certain what's happening. If there's one thing he hates, it's not knowing what I'm doing.
In my defense, I'm not sure myself what is going on.
My phone's ringing!
It's Ed.
What should I do? What would I even say at this point?
I'm not ready to talk to him yet. If I reject the call though, he will blow it out of proportion and read too much into it. But if I leave it to ring, that will piss him off too.
I'm in catch 22 really and I don't even have a plan.
"This might be above my job description, but does the other half make a habit of causing a scene?", asked the driver.
At this point I was already immersed in a conversation with my own thoughts, I was not in the mood for passing

questions from people that frankly wouldn't be as quick to talk with me about solving my problems.

I answered him anyway, perhaps not in the way he expected. "If you're keen to exceed the responsibilities of your role, perhaps you should pay more attention to the upkeep of this vehicle than business that doesn't concern you!"

"Of course. My apologies."

It was silent for a second.

"The car isn't that bad, is it?", he followed jokingly.

"No. I'm sorry, I have had a day like you wouldn't believe and it's only 4pm. I shouldn't have taken it out on you, the car is… great."

I tried to pick the tone up in my voice, but I know I still sounded flat. I wonder if it sounded sarcastic. He probably thinks I'm a cow.

Ed was ringing again, and I could see he had text too.

I knew I couldn't keep staring at the phone, it was only making me feel more anxious.

I switched it on silent but the light from my phone kept triggering from the messages Ed was sending through.

That curious part of me wanted to read them but knew it was pointless. It would only end in conflict and I don't think I could handle that right now. Ellie needed me to be as balanced as mentally possible right now in a situation like this.

"My wife. She runs group therapy sessions. I have a habit of taking a little more interest than I probably should in the life of others, she's sort of rubbed off on me like that. I apologise for probing about your business but if it's all the same, I hope

SOME PEOPLE AREN'T MEANT TO BE SAVED

you and your girl are okay."
I looked at him through the rear-view mirror and smiled a little. It was nice I guess for someone to try and understand my perspective and feelings, even if it was a brief encounter with a stranger.
I sound so pathetic.
I speak like there has never been a good moment shared between Ed and I.
Of course, there has been.
In fact, we've shared many.
Oh Alice, what if you're just blowing everything out of proportion because you're a paranoid wreck. Ed would have been okay once he got back home, he's battling an addiction for Christ's sake, of course he's going to be stressed more than usual. None of this is going to help things at all, why didn't I think all of this through properly? Things would only be worse if I turned back now.
Well, worse than things had to be.
Today was a scare yes but to just leave like that, without a word, taking Ellie, no note. I'd probably be pissed too.
This is messed up and once again I'm at the centre of it all.
Speaking of Ed, my phone hasn't lit up with a text or call for a short while.
Is it weird that I find that strange?
Paranoia - what did I tell you. I just can't shake it. Everyone has a habit though I suppose.
"Sorry to disturb you, but which end of Chelmsford am I heading to?"
Was it so obvious I was distracted?

SOME PEOPLE AREN'T MEANT TO BE SAVED

It took me a few seconds to twig, but I answered.
"How far away are we?"
"Not far now love, I reckon another 15 minutes depending on traffic."
I could see him looking at me through the rear-view mirror. I avoided making eye contact.
I always do to be honest. It's my way of avoiding an overflow of conversation with people I don't know. Not to mention the fact that my anxiety is through the roof right about now trying to prepare for what awaits and how long it will take me before I come to my senses.
The car seemed to be making more turns, maybe we're close. The area looks much quieter than the one we are used to. I don't know if that improves the situation or makes it worse. I appreciate a little white noise from time to time - it's a different noise to get lost in, away from my thoughts. Music helps me too strangely. Honestly, I have a playlist for everything.
I'm drawn away from my thoughts by the numbing sensation taking over my left arm. I hadn't even noticed that Ellie had fallen asleep.
She definitely won't sleep tonight now.
The taxi began to slow so I tried to wake Ellie gently. Of course, she was showing no signs of co-operation though, instead she fell into my lap and hugged my legs.
"Are we here?"
"A little further down this road and you will be, love".
It hit me. I didn't have anything on me apart from keys. I left my purse in the kitchen drawer at home. I didn't even bring

my bank card with me. I must have thought the cheque was enough, I don't know, but it certainly isn't going to cover our fare. I've been rude as well, so he is definitely going to be less likely to understand the situation.

Fuck's sake Alice. Ed always tells me I'm a stupid bitch. I guess I'll start realizing that a lot more now if I'm planning to flit for good.

I really haven't thought this through at all.

"We're here love, now you can yell at me again if you like," he chuckles calmly, "but I take it this is your first time in the area?"

I knew he thought I was rude.

I looked at him and started crying. I don't know where it came from.

It wasn't dramatic or anything. Actually, I was just sort of looking at him wide eyed, and they just… rolled down my cheeks.

My mouth went to speak but it just didn't.

Ellie was still asleep on my lap and I still couldn't muster the words to tell him I couldn't pay.

The whole thing was a mess. I felt like my best option was to ask him to drive us back. At least that way I could avoid disrupting another innocent person's day all because I couldn't cope.

I'm stronger than this. Or so everyone else says. Why should Ed be sitting at home wracking his brains as to why he just had to watch his wife and daughter drive away in a taxi? Why should Ellie be asleep on my knee in the back of a taxi outside the house of a man she doesn't know - or myself even? And why should this gentleman drive home empty-handed?

"I'm really sorry, I know it's a lot to ask especially after I was so rude as well but is there any chance you could take us back to the address you picked us up from?"

He turned the car off at this point and turned to face me. We made eye contact for a moment. Then I stared out the windscreen. I don't even think I was blinking.

"Driving back would not be at all a lot to ask, it's what I do and actually I would be thankful for the extra money…"

"Great"

"But! I would not feel comfortable earning extra money if it meant going against my better judgement and potentially putting you in harm's way. I think you came here for a reason and that you should respect whatever your better judgement was trying to tell you in the moment too."

It went silent for a moment. It felt like a Deja vu moment and I suddenly realised why. My mother was a wise woman for advice. I can't say I took it all at times but that's what kids do isn't it - they rebel and try to find their own way to make their mark on life.

He continued, "Even if you stay for a few hours or days until whatever that was settles down. It can't do any more harm surely?"

He had a point, for a man that knew absolutely nothing about the situation. Still didn't settle the fact I had no way of paying him but at this point I don't think it could get any worse. Or awkward either to be honest.

"Thank you for that, you're right. Space would be the

healthiest option right now"
"Spot on. My wife always says, no matter where you are, the force of the wind will be felt if it is forecasted. But she also says a wise person knows when to seek shelter for the duration to avoid feeling its full force."
"So, heading back now would be like?"
"Heading for the tide. Let the storm pass first."
I don't feel like I'm sitting in a taxi. More of a therapy room. I don't know him or his wife for that matter, but I feel like I know them both now. I honestly feel like this conversation has given me the strength to get through the next thirty minutes at least. If only for that, I owe it to cut this conversation short and let him know I can't pay.
"You have honestly helped me believe I can push through these next few hours, which makes me feel even worse"
"Oh?" He looks confused.
"No, I don't mean it like that. Sorry. I'm just going to get to the point and say I honestly left with nothing. No purse. No bag. Nothing. I have money, but not physically, is there any way you can stop by tomorrow? I'm not sure if I'll still be here, but…"
"Sure, just ring the office when you get a chance and you can pay over the phone. I'll leave a note on the system, no problem. I'll jot a number down here for you…"
He looked up at me in pause. I was unsure what for, then he said, "your name, love?"
"Hope".
I don't know where it came from, but it was too late to take it back.

SOME PEOPLE AREN'T MEANT TO BE SAVED

I even said it again. I felt like such an idiot, but I was laughing somewhere inside. Kicking myself on the opposite side somewhere in there too.
"Lovely name. Well, Hope, take this and ring the number on the card when you're ready."
I smiled at him briefly and rubbed Ellie's nose.
"Come on baby, we're here, wake up", I said putting the card into my inner pocket.
Ellie rubbed her eyes as she woke. Bless her. I hate waking her up. I remember how much I hated it when I was younger. We got out of the taxi and walked up to our temporary accommodation.
"Change of plan Ell. We're going to be here for a few hours and then we're going to go home, okay?"
"Why Mummy? Is Aunty Lee Busy?"
I knelt down next to her and held her hands.
"We're not at Aunty Lee's yet, baby, mummy is going to get in touch with her. We will talk about it properly later baby but for now let's go in and see what we can find to do yes?"
She looked up from the ground and grinned. I knew what she wanted to do straight away.
"You can have fun anywhere mummy, daddy always says that". She didn't stop grinning. I giggled with her for a moment.
"Exactly and he's right when he says that but no Queen of the Castle here Ell's, they aren't our sofas, okay?"
"Yes, mummy", she sighed.
The drive was long and full of all sorts of thoughts and while today was difficult, I knew the hardest part was yet to come.

SOME PEOPLE AREN'T MEANT TO BE SAVED

Time to get through these next few hours.
Wish me luck.

SOME PEOPLE AREN'T MEANT TO BE SAVED

THE FIRST BIT

If today has taught me anything, it's that I definitely swear too much. I can't help it. It has become a natural response to unexpected events.
Some people cry, I swear.
I cry too of course but since having Ellie, crying is usually a private party that I have to make time for.
Not that I'm implying swearing is a healthy substitute for crying. It obviously isn't. Well not in this generation anyway.
Swearing is still seen as an ill-mannered trait.
Then there's Ed too of course.
There used to be a time where he would jump to console me when I cried but these days, he can't stand it and I don't mean because he can't stand to see me upset.
I mean because it stresses him out.
It doesn't make any sense to me but then again, we're two quite different people and I always try to understand that.
But at least now you don't think I'm some cold-hearted bitch

with no emotion. I've just worked hard to preserve myself and hide things.
It might sound crazy to you and that's okay. It just works for me.
Less hassle.
Being in someone else's home today was weird. Not that it wasn't nice. It just wasn't my home.
I'm not used to everything being on one floor either.
It didn't seem to faze Ellie; she was off exploring the minute we stepped through the door.
I envy the innocence of the child's mind.
I noticed I walked sort of slowly as I entered. I still didn't feel confident in my decision to leave home. I was surrounded by pictures on the wall of faces I didn't know, too much space and little sound.
I sound ungrateful, I know.
I don't mean to, but if I'm being honest, I don't feel grateful either. I know it sounds bad but it's the truth. I don't know how to feel, I just feel numb. All I want is to be at home - now more than ever.
"MUMMY!" Shouted Ellie.
My heart sank. I ran through into the front room, but she wasn't there.
"Ellie!"
I found her standing at the back doors of the conservatory, smiling. I stood next to her.
"It's like they knew you were coming right?' I said winking and smiling.
"Can I Mum? Please?"

SOME PEOPLE AREN'T MEANT TO BE SAVED

"Hmm, I don't know about that. I'll think about it if you promise to be extra good today, deal?"
"Deal mummy!"
She loves swings.
I'm glad there was something here that made her feel comfortable. It made me feel more grounded knowing that she was okay. It gave me a chance to think for a second.
The kitchen was... big!
It made me think of Mum's kitchen. She was forever in there. Cooking and baking.
There was a handwritten note hanging on the fridge. It had my name on it.
I didn't want to read it at first, I just felt a bit uneasy. I mean how much do I really know about this Pete character really? Nonetheless, I've walked into his house, no questions asked and, with my daughter too.
Argh! Why can't I just focus my mind on one problem at a time?
I feel so overwhelmed by everything and the peace doesn't help as much as I thought.
Okay Alice. Pull yourself together for Christ's sake.
I pulled the note from the fridge and read it.
Fuck-sake.
I mean it's not bad news, more a change of plan.
A drastic change to the plan if I'm allowed to say.
I just don't get it. Maybe I don't need to read too much into it, but I can't help but.
The cheque was going to bounce, but Pete had left £4000 cash hidden in his bedside table. He said it would help me

SOME PEOPLE AREN'T MEANT TO BE SAVED

'stay under radar' if that's what I wanted.

I wouldn't have to pay rent so practically speaking, I could make this stretch for a few months. That's if I had plans to stay.

Even if I did though, how do I know I would be able to secure our finances thereafter? How do I know if I'll be ready to work? What if I need more time? What if time isn't even the answer?

The gentleman in the taxi spoke some wise words but he didn't know our situation. He would have probably advised me differently if I had given him more insight, but I hate the thought of unintentionally painting Ed to be a bad soul.

I know I haven't had a lot of time to think but time isn't exactly on my side. We've already been here for an hour. Maybe I could take Ellie and I for some food before we head home.

Ed is going to be outraged anyway, there's no doubt about that. In fact, I think his mood would only worsen the longer we were away. I don't know how I feel about that, but I can't just avoid it.

Going for food and doing something normal might help to calm my nerves a little so I can gather my thoughts.

It will help me feel more in Mum mode too instead of me mode. When I'm in Mum mode I make better decisions.

No one tells you how hard it is to be a Mum while you're battling your hardest moments in life. But she's the reason I'm still here and the reason I'll continue to try.

I wonder if Pete would mind if I altered the plan a little. Going home today would be better than dragging it out.

SOME PEOPLE AREN'T MEANT TO BE SAVED

If I go home with money in my pocket, that's got to relieve some of the tension. It would definitely solve a couple of problems.

Things have only been a little more stressful lately because Ed lost his job. He needs me to support him right now, not abandon him.

"Ellie, you scared me silly."

She disturbed my train of thought. I thought she was still on the swing.

"Mummy someone's at the door"

"What? Are you sure baby? Mummy didn't hear anything?"

Then again, I was lost in my own world.

I walked toward the kitchen door but hesitated from walking into the hallway entirely.

I could see a shadow through the glass of the door.

If I can see them, maybe they could see me?

I backed off into the kitchen.

I don't know why. I'm nowhere near home, nobody knows I'm here. Ed surely wouldn't have been able to find me, would he?

All of a sudden, I feel sick, and the paranoia starts kicking off again.

I turned around and Ellie had gone.

Why does there have to be all these doorways from room to room.

I peered through the second doorway to the conservatory and gestured to Ellie to stay quiet.

The door went again.

This was ridiculous, I had to answer.

SOME PEOPLE AREN'T MEANT TO BE SAVED

Whoever it was obviously wasn't in a rush to leave.
As I walked to the door, pins and needles kicked in tenfold and my mouth was dry.
I unlocked the door and opened it slightly. Enough to see half my body but no more than that.
For a split second I thought Ed was going to boot the door open, ranting and raving, but it wasn't him.
I wasn't any more relieved to see a stranger though if I'm honest.
"I saw you and your little one head in from your taxi. You must be family?" said the gentleman.
I think he could tell I was confused.
"Sorry, I haven't introduced myself, have I? My wife and I have lived next door to Pete for 5 years now. We were sad to hear about his final days in the hospice. How are you holding up?"
I wasn't sure if he was being nosey or genuinely trying to show support. Either way, I don't even have the capacity for my own problems at the moment, never mind someone else's.
Again, no offence intended.
Shouldering other people's problems used to work as a distraction from my own problems for a while. Not so much now.
"It's really nice that you took the time to come over and I wouldn't want to be rude but we're only here for a couple more hours and we would really appreciate the alone time right about now. Sorry, I really don't mean to be rude."
I felt awful as I was saying it.

SOME PEOPLE AREN'T MEANT TO BE SAVED

I just wanted to find the quickest way to shut the door.
I'm never in the mood for my own neighbours, I'm certainly not in the mood to inherit anymore.
"Absolutely, don't feel rude. I can imagine you need your space. You know where we are if we can help in anyway" he said.
I smiled subtly and thanked him then closed the door.
I stood behind it for a moment and inhaled deeply and rolled my eyes.
I could hear Ellie giggling somewhere.
I headed towards the front room to find her jumping all over the sofa.
 She just doesn't listen to me.
The first thing I said before we stepped foot through the door was, 'no Queen of the castle'.
I stood and stared at her, but she just carried on.
"Get off the sofa Ellie", I yelled sternly. "How many times do I have to tell you things before you actually listen? And, if you think you're playing on that swing now you've got another thing coming. Kitchen. Now"
"Mummy, why are you shouting?", Ellie said.
"I wouldn't have to if you just listened to me. This isn't our house, Ellie. These aren't our sofas, carpets, walls, beds. Nothing, Ellie. Respect that, please"
She got down from the sofa and walked into the kitchen and sat on the bar stool and slumped her arms on the island.
Of course, I feel awful now.
The last thing I wanted to do was snap at Ellie. None of this is her fault.

SOME PEOPLE AREN'T MEANT TO BE SAVED

I stroked her head as I walked past and sat next to her.
"I'm sorry baby. Sometimes Mummy reacts before thinking and that's wrong. I shouldn't have shouted at you. Of course, it was still naughty of you to jump on the sofa especially after Mummy asked you not to. But there is always a better way to communicate things and I should have spoken with you differently. I'm sorry for that. Do you think maybe you could forgive me - even just a little bit?"
"It depends, Mummy"
"I thought you might say that, so how does eating out sound?"
"Can I have an ice cream?"
"Mhmm, two scoops"
"Deal Mummy."
I'm glad she was smiling again.
I'll make it up to her when we're home and sort things with Ed.
I hadn't checked my phone since leaving. I haven't felt like I've had the time or head space to be honest.
I wish I hadn't checked it either.
Ed had called thirty-three times. He'd sent twenty-five messages.
I honestly felt sick.
I felt a lot of other things too, but I don't feel there are any ways to put into words just how weak I felt.
For a second, I thought about leaving food and just heading home to prevent prolonging the situation, but I couldn't let Ellie down.
I thought about sending a text but everything I typed sounded

SOME PEOPLE AREN'T MEANT TO BE SAVED

provoking.
Not to me, but I know Ed. He interprets things differently.
Not to say it's out of the ordinary.
Of course, there'll be others too.
He can't help the way he has come to make sense of the world and everything in it. I just wish he would realise it isn't mine either.
Things are bad already, right? Staying out a while later surely couldn't aggravate the situation anymore, could it? Plus, if we go for food, we'll have something to show for our time away.
I could keep the receipt. Maybe I could play it like I needed a bit of airtime and hadn't checked my phone?
Ahh, but I left my purse at home, didn't I?
How am I even going to explain the money to him?
Maybe he won't care once he sees it?
I'm just going to have to take it as it comes. I don't really have a choice, do I?
I went to open his messages but stopped suddenly.
If I opened them, he wouldn't believe that I hadn't seen any of his messages.
He is the type to check let's bear in mind.
All I could do at this point was push through time and deal with whatever unfolded as and when it came.
So, we went for food and talked.
Ellie actually told me that this was the 'best day' she'd had in ages. The moment was short but precious. I felt like a Mum in a different way when I heard that.
My role has become consumed by my desire to shelter her.

SOME PEOPLE AREN'T MEANT TO BE SAVED

The last few months, Ed's behaviour has sort of been a bit more unpredictable. His addiction has gotten worse. He denies it, but it has.
Things took a sharp turn when Ellie turned one, but like I said Ed always tries to mind himself in Ellie's company.
But lately. I don't know. It gets harder to understand him the longer we're together.
It's like he dislikes me more and more with each year that passes by. I don't know how to explain it in a way that makes sense. It's like a love, hate thing. Where the balance gets distorted, and he starts hating me more with each year that passes and loves me less.
When I try to talk to him about it, he just rolls his eyes.
'You really need to stop being so insecure Alice', he'd say.
'Believe what you want', he'd say.
I just wanted him to be interested in knowing why I was feeling the way I was.
I wanted him to care.
When I think about it, even though I've been scattered, this was actually the best day I've had in a while too.
I can't remember the last time we had spare change to eat out for food.
I cuddled Ellie and smiled. She hugged me too.
I was smiling because for the first time in ages, I felt like a proper Mum.
Ellie and I have done something normal and enjoyed it.
I did that.
I made her smile.
We stood outside waiting for our taxi home.

SOME PEOPLE AREN'T MEANT TO BE SAVED

I felt ready to face Ed.
I was ready to face him as Ellie's Mum.
We need to be positive influences in her life and that's exactly what he needs to hear. It's not about us. It's about her.
I swore my child would have the family he or she deserved before Ellie arrived. I didn't want to be that broken family people gossip about.
I wanted us to be strong and push through anything life threw at us.
Both he and Ellie needed me right now. Maybe I just needed to toughen up.
The longer I've been away, the more I've been able to think. A lot of it is full of paranoia, yes. But it's helping me to reflect and ask myself healthy questions anyone in my situation would ask.
I think.
The taxi pulled up and Ellie raced on in.
We usually walk or get the bus everywhere.
I was feeling a bit sick, but I hadn't lost sight of what needed to happen. I just hope he doesn't overreact. The last time he did, I couldn't leave the house for weeks. I had bruises you just couldn't cover and, I'm still waiting for someone to write a book on perfect excuses for nosey, judgmental, bastards. Staying in was just the easier option. I've got used to taking those.
Not now though.
This time, things had to be different.
If I didn't break the cycle sometime, when was I going to?

SOME PEOPLE AREN'T MEANT TO BE SAVED

When was I going to stop taking the easy routes?
Maybe I've been looking at things wrong this whole time. I've been thinking that the easiest thing to do would be to avoid going home, right? Because I'm avoiding conflict. I'm avoiding taking accountability for my actions.
But now, another part of my brain feels like it's just woken up.
All of a sudden, I thought, maybe the easy option is to go home.
It's what I know. It's what I've known for eight years.
Well, I've got to know more of this side of Ed over the last four year to be exact.
It just makes sense to always go back or be there. We've been together since I was nineteen, and him twenty-one. I wouldn't even know how to start a new life.
Not without him.
So now my brain is like 'actually Alice the best decision is not always the easy one or the route you know, instead it's the route you don't. Sometimes making unexpected decisions is the best option you have available'.
"Ellie, did you like the apartment we stayed in before with the swing in the garden?"
"You know I did Mummy", Ellie grinned.
"What would you say to staying for a few nights? Like a girls' only holiday", I said excitedly.
She gasped.
I thought I was going to have to hold her jaw up! She loved the idea.
So, we came back.

SOME PEOPLE AREN'T MEANT TO BE SAVED

By now, you'll understand my personality more - I hope - so you'll know I wasn't as confident in my decision as it might read.
What were Pete's neighbours going to think?
I told one we were only staying a few hours. I hope they don't knock on out of curiosity when we're back.
I didn't know what I was going to do about Ed. Should I text or call?
Obviously, I had to do something, but I really didn't want to think about that right now.
I almost forgot about paying for the taxi here too. I mentally reminded myself to sort that once we had settled.
We stopped by a local supermarket to grab some pyjamas, washing bits, clothes and essentials, on the way. We might have got some goodies too. I wanted to try to make it a little special for Ellie.
I wasn't in the right mood to be hosting a vacation, but she deserved to feel special.
I'm not really prepared for anything ahead and I can't predict the outcome. But, for now, I get to be Ellie's Mum for a few nights and make her feel special. Mummy's pampered princess.
I turned the T.V on as soon as we got back. Just for a bit of normality to be honest. I even switched the hoover on. Not to hoover. Just for some familiarity.
It felt odd, but it helped.
White noise works for grown-ass adults too. Don't think that shit works just on babies.
Anyway, it wasn't long before I remembered I had to sort

that payment for the taxi.
I left Ellie with her snacks on the sofa and went into the kitchen. I had difficulties remembering what I did with the card the driver gave me.
I definitely took it.
I didn't have a bag.
I checked the inner pocket on my jacket, where I keep my phone, and it was there.
It was a bit of a strange moment actually. The card he wrote the number on was for the support group his wife must organise.
Why did he write it there? Did he not have anything else to hand or was that his attempt at being subtle? Domestic abuse?
That's a bit forward, I thought.
What an offense to people who actually experience real abuse?
Ed's behaviour isn't consistent. It isn't well thought out. It isn't rational.
He battles a debilitating addiction, in my opinion. One where the odds constantly feel stacked against him.
He really has struggled.
He was amazing when we first met. He just got wrapped up in over protecting me once I got pregnant.
It's getting harder to go back to the beginning really.
My mind wonders if maybe it's because I choose to avoid having that conversation with myself.
To face it, I'd have to be ready for change and I don't think I am. Not mentally. It's going to be hard work. Too much work

SOME PEOPLE AREN'T MEANT TO BE SAVED

than I had time for.
We're talking years of rewriting here.
Years of erasing.
No more editing. The story has ended. The end. Then what? New book?
My mind has just been so closed up to now and I think I've realised that the more I've been writing.
If you're wondering about what I did about the taxi before I got lost in another train of thought, I rang them.
The lady on the switchboard said the fare had actually been covered.
I was confused, as you can probably imagine.
I hadn't paid. The only person that would have thought to have covered the fare would be the driver himself. But why give me the card and the number if he had no intentions of letting me cover the fare?
That's when I realised he obviously intended to give me the card and maybe the easiest way for him, without offending me, was like that? I don't know.
But now I'm sitting here writing this down with all sorts of thoughts and worries.
It's late now and Ellie is asleep.
We're in the same room. I don't think I could cope with us sleeping apart in a house we don't know after the day we've had. I wanted her close.
It was nice to see her asleep, looking peaceful and content. I giggled a couple of times at some of the facial expressions she was pulling but she still looked beautiful.
Children aren't for everyone and people need to be okay with

SOME PEOPLE AREN'T MEANT TO BE SAVED

that. I just can't stress that enough.

But for me, Ellie has been my saving grace. She's been my hope and my comfort. She's, my purpose.

It's been nice to spend some time with her this evening. It's hard to stay focused at home these days, so to give her some happy Mum time was the highlight of my day.

I still wasn't any organised in my plan moving forward.

I know; I've avoided it.

You're probably rolling your eyes because it's taken me till now to figure out.

I wouldn't blame you, but it was nice to find out by myself. I looked in a drawer next to the bed to see if I could find any paper and a pen.

I came across a hospital letter.

I felt awful for prying, but I read it. It hit me that I never asked Pete much about his diagnosis. We were always so caught up in what was going on in my life. I felt selfish for a moment and guilty too. He had been battling this for some time. What a selfless man.

We'd been writing for a while and it's only now I realised the reason I knew less about him is because he was always so concerned with making sure I had someone to talk to. He never applied any pressure with advice I wouldn't take. He didn't assume to know my situation or pass judgement. I liked that about him. He always wanted to understand my way of thinking. It interested him. It was nice to have someone want to listen to me for a change and maybe I took advantage of that.

I found a pen and an already-written-on piece of paper.

SOME PEOPLE AREN'T MEANT TO BE SAVED

I wrote Ed's name at the top.
I was trying to write down any and all ways I could think of, to move forward maturely. Or at least buy me some thinking time.
I definitely don't want to slap a victim label on my head, but I definitely think time would be good. It would give me time to figure out exactly what this is.
I've been around the houses and back today, and while some thoughts haven't been worth a moment in my mind, each one has at the very least helped me dig deeper and look at the situation from other perspectives.
My train of thought jumped to think of Lisa. I wanted so badly to ring her. She's my big sister. I felt like I needed her right about now.
I started ringing but I bottled it.
I hung up after the first ring.
I just felt too anxious about it all.
She'll probably be pissed that I'm ringing just to ask for something after all this time.
Why does everyone always seem to have that person that stands by them no matter what? That person that jumps to their rescue.
Everyone except me. Or so it feels.
I've been given a lot of advice over the years, but nothing actually prepares you for the harsh reality of adulthood that advice can't protect you from.
I just wish I had someone I felt I could turn to without judgement at times of need.
Bloody hell!

SOME PEOPLE AREN'T MEANT TO BE SAVED

My phone was ringing.
It was Lisa!
My heart started racing. I couldn't bring myself to answer so I just let it ring.
I hadn't had time to think it through, I didn't know what I was going to say to her. I still didn't know why I was ringing!
She started calling again.
I was a little confused but still no more curious enough to answer.
I pressed reject. I thought about sending a message to say it was an accident, but she beat me to it.
She sent a message saying, 'You obviously called for a reason, answer'. Before I had a chance to reply, she rang again.
"Hey Lee," I tried to sound positive, but she saw through me.
"Alice, I know you're doing that voice. That one where you try to play it cool. What's going on? It's late, you know?" she said.
"I know that Lisa".
It went silent for a little. I just wanted to hang up to be honest.
"Ellie and I have gone away for a little girly time. I know we haven't spoken in a while, but I was just wondering if you could say we were staying with you for a few days if anyone asked?"
"Who asked?", she said impatiently.
"Ed…" She jumped in before I had a chance to say anything else.
"Why would you ask me to do that? That's a little strange,

SOME PEOPLE AREN'T MEANT TO BE SAVED

don't you think?"
"Why do you always have to psychoanalyse everything Lisa?"
"Still the same old Alice then,"
"Do you know what, forget I asked. If you can't do it, it's fine"
"Let me guess, you'll hang up now even though I've heard nothing from you for the last four years"
"I'm not in the mood for your insensitive, bitchy little comments. I called because I thought that maybe I could come to you for help. I'll ask someone else."
"Wait!", said Lisa.
It went silent again until she said, "I just have to say one last thing okay and then we'll leave it there…" I let her continue, "You actually made the first bitchy remark, but you're right"
She agreed to be my alibi if Ed called to ask.
But it was hard to convince her to let sleeping dogs lie as far as 'why?' was concerned.
She's not going to let it rest but for now I felt relieved to have just ticked one drama off my list.
Now just to sort the main bit. The Ed bit.
I fell back onto the bed and stared at the ceiling hoping that some god, any god, would just help me out here. Obviously, I knew it wasn't going to help so I picked my phone up and scrolled through my contacts.
I scrolled past the names of people that I used to know to get to Ed's name but when I got there, I just stared at it. I could picture his face as he got my text. How angry he would be. No doubt punch something or do something silly.

SOME PEOPLE AREN'T MEANT TO BE SAVED

Argh!
Then the phone calls would fire my way, followed by texts. It would honestly be less effort to go back.
I really couldn't bring myself to ring him and hear his voice. The thought just made me sick to my stomach.
I'm not sure why yet but it's something else to think about.
I started texting him, but I just couldn't find the right words. Was there even a right way to say that his family wasn't returning for a few days?
All the same, I started typing and just tried to continue with caution.
'Ed, I'm sorry. You must be going out of your mind. I don't know how to say what I'm about to say without you getting angry. Stressing you out is the last thing I want after how hard things have been recently. But right now, I thought the healthiest thing for us both would be to have some space. Me and Ellie have come to stay with my sister for a few days. Oh, and I'll sort the house, Lee's going to borrow us the money. Please don't be angry, love you"
It took me a good ten minutes on average to press send, I think. It could have been longer to be honest but at least I did it.
I can't believe I made it through the first day to be honest, but the real challenge will always be tomorrow. I can't imagine myself catching much sleep tonight, but I'll have to try.
My phone vibrated as I rolled over.
I felt lightheaded. I wasn't reading it, not tonight.
I should have expected him to still be up. Waiting.

SOME PEOPLE AREN'T MEANT TO BE SAVED

Looks like it's tomorrow's problem. I'm switching my phone off and putting the pen down.
Hopefully, I wake up with the same mindset. Don't have high hopes, though.

SOME PEOPLE AREN'T MEANT TO BE SAVED

CHANGE

I didn't sleep much. I was comfy but I still tossed and turned a lot. I think I had a few hours but even when my eyes were closed, I still felt like part of me hadn't fully fallen asleep.
I remember opening my eyes often.
I felt strange when I woke up. I forgot I wasn't at home for the first few minutes.
I felt weirder the longer time passed in the morning.
I tried to make the atmosphere more normal. I put the news on, but the background noise just wasn't working today. Nothing was drowning out my urge to want to hide away, but I knew that would only make me worse.
Ellie was slumped in front of the T.V all morning. I won't lie, I was thankful she made the morning easier; I don't think I could have managed a morning of play.
I spent a few hours trying to convince myself I needed to lift my spirits. I couldn't just drag myself through the day, it

wouldn't be fair on Ellie.
I tried to talk to her.
I know she's only five but sometimes I think it's a good thing to include her in making decisions.
I value what she thinks and sometimes her ideas are better than mine.
She really is the calm to my storm.
I asked her what she thought about the trip so far and it was a surprise to hear how much she was still enjoying it.
She thought that we were lucky to live like princesses for a little bit. She said it made her excited to be 'bigger'.
Bless her.
Sometimes I try to imagine her as she gets older and it's exciting to imagine all the little things like how she will look, what she'll be doing, whether she'll be happy.
Then the worry sets in.
What if she encounters tough experiences in her life like I have? I know I can't shelter her, but I can't think of a better alternative either.
There has to be another way that I can prevent her from crossing paths with the same sort of love that's found me.
I'm twenty-seven now and I still remember what it was like to be a 'young adult'.
It was tough.
I've been bullied.
I've been ridiculed for the colour of my skin and told in the same breath I couldn't use it as an excuse for the way I've been treated.
I've been disappointed.

SOME PEOPLE AREN'T MEANT TO BE SAVED

I've been scared.
I've played the bitch too, I won't lie. I'm ashamed to say it but if we can't be honest with ourselves, who can we be honest with?
I was learning.
It's not an excuse, it's a statement.
I've sponged up all sorts of behaviours over the years and manifested them in my personal life, so I know how hard it can be to shake them off. But I've grown.
The thing is, we all have our bad moments; some are just more reluctant to admit it than others. We all make mistakes. Some wrongs we can never right, and we just have to accept that. What matters is what you do thereafter.
Can you fix it? Or do you leave it to evolve into every area of your personality until you're just another prick, raising more pricks for the generations to come?
Somewhere along the line something has to change.
Ellie thinks her dad and I are like the Mummy's and Daddy's she reads about in her stories and draws about in her pictures. How do I tell her we're not before she finds out for herself?
But back to the point… I'm grateful for her innocence.
I just know it's going to be hard to watch her grow up and not interfere.
No matter which way I look, I feel stuck.
I have been able to hear myself think more since being here, which is something I'm not all too used to. But what was I going to do?
I felt like shit. Honestly.
How was I going to dig myself out of the current situation

SOME PEOPLE AREN'T MEANT TO BE SAVED

that was our life?

It was down to me to set an example but, being blunt, all I was doing was showing her was how to put up with shit. Have I been demonstrating strength, or weakness? I can't decide.

Parent's day is always a big fat reminder of what bad examples we are.

You know what Mum's are like in the playground and the cliquey relationships they build with teachers. Always on stand-by for playground gossip and hear-say antics. The biggest mouths and the tone-deaf voices. It's like they're taken back in time every time they're on the playground.

I know I'm being mean now; it has just sucked to be me for such a long time, and I feel so angry at the world. I'm not usually a cow, I'm not sure why I'm snapping so much lately.

I don't even feel like me anymore.

I don't even think I quite like myself most days. I'm always so down and envious of everyone. I wished my life were as picture perfect as theirs.

I think I've just got used to feeling angry. Living with Ed has really encouraged that habit, I'll be honest. The household is always tense, it's gotten sort of hard to not be on my toes in that sense.

The rest of the day was sort of boring to be honest, we had to nip out for more essentials, but that was about it.

The more time passed, I realised I had been avoiding checking my phone.

I started to feel a little more grounded and I just didn't want

SOME PEOPLE AREN'T MEANT TO BE SAVED

anything to interrupt that I guess.
Then Ellie started asking questions about her dad and things just started to fall in on me again.
I think I was chasing a fantasy I was living out in my head, but it was going to come crashing down at some point.
The subject was easy to deflect but I knew I had to get in touch.
I actually made our evening meal tonight, so I decided I would get in touch after that.
Though when I checked, I was confused.
I had loads of texts and calls but not just from Ed.
Lisa had been calling too.
I felt sick.
I didn't know where to start or what message to check first.
Between them both I had fourty-seven texts alone.
Then a message popped up to say I had a voicemail.
My head was blown, and I just couldn't cope with being me.
I wanted to be someone else; anyone else, even just for a minute.
I tried to focus on Ellie and started opening Ed's message.
His texts were quite calm at first. He even apologises too for flying off the handle about the letter.
All of a sudden, I felt guilty.
I didn't want to read the rest, but I did anyway. I felt like maybe now might be a good time to go home if he was like this.
Maybe this has helped him see sense about the way things have been?
Maybe the old him is trying to fight for us?

SOME PEOPLE AREN'T MEANT TO BE SAVED

I lost those thoughts soon after though.
He started getting aggressive, promising to call the police, questioning my state of mind.
I couldn't believe what I was reading. I was actually doubting myself for a second.
I still am now if we're allowing honesty here.
You're probably doubting me too but please believe me when I say my state of mind is intact. I might be a little thrown by the current circumstances, but anyone in my position would be, wouldn't they?
Cheeky bastard has the nerve to question my sanity.
This is exactly what I mean.
The environment is toxic, and the thing is, everything I say is 'wrong'. In fact, I'm so used to being 'wrong' I just keep my mouth fucking shut.
Maybe that's why I'm starting to snap more?
Maybe I've just had enough too.
He's not the only one that's allowed to be fed up.
Why can't we understand each other?
I'm tired of putting my feelings to one side all the time.
I'm not asking for Ed to always agree with me but just to hear me out at the very least, surely, I'm not expecting much.
Some of his last texts didn't make sense.
I was definitely missing something.
It cannot be coincidental either that I've had multiple texts from both him and my sister.
I just hope nothing bad has happened.
I feel awful for doubting Ed, but I'm hoping you'll understand why I might be?

SOME PEOPLE AREN'T MEANT TO BE SAVED

I checked the texts from Lee and I really wanted to give up. I had so many texts…
'Alice, call me as soon as you get this. Ed's been on the phone wanting to speak to you', 'Why is your phone off?', 'Alice I don't think I can stall him much longer?', 'Alice this is freaking me out now.'
I was too overwhelmed.
I told Ed space would be good.
Lee will be asking all sorts of questions now, why couldn't he just respect and give me the space we both needed? I'm tired of feeling sick to my stomach, worrying about what's next. I'm not sure how much more I can take.
I still had a voicemail to check from Ed and even though I couldn't stomach it, I knew I had to find out what was going on.
He was screaming.
I've never heard him like that.
I shut the kitchen door. I know Ellie wouldn't have been able to hear but it made me feel better.
He didn't believe we were at Lisa's, how on earth was I going to fix this?
For the first time in a while, I was starting to feel like I finally had a grip on the steering wheel - metaphorically speaking. Like I was starting to think for myself.
Nothing ever goes right. I'm starting to feel like this was all pointless.
I just didn't have the strength to face dealing with it all now. My mood had already dropped.
I just can't cope with any more shit right now. I put my phone

SOME PEOPLE AREN'T MEANT TO BE SAVED

in the kitchen drawer and left it there for a few hours.
Ellie and I cuddled up on the sofa and watched two films. It was a nice way to spend time with her silently. I know it sounds awful, but I didn't know what else to do.
Time was dragging and I couldn't stop thinking about what I was going to do.
Ellie fell asleep on the sofa a little earlier than usual.
It's weird. She seems to be comfortable here.
Me on the other hand, not so much. All I can think about is home and going back.
Ed wouldn't be willing to leave for a little though. No chance.
Anyway, I carried Ellie to bed and headed toward the kitchen so I wouldn't wake her.
I had an idea.
It sounded more and more crazy the more I relayed it to myself but it's the only plan I had.
I must have taken about ten deep breaths before I even picked the phone up.
"Lee, I've not long turned my phone on. Ellie and I have been out all day. You said Ed called?"
"Alice, whatever is going on you have got to be straight with me. Ed said some things and…"
"What do you mean Ed said some things?"
"Alice. What is going on?"
I was panicking at this point. Why wasn't she answering any of my questions? "Alice!"
"Lee everything is fine, I'm simply confused. Is Ed, okay? What's going on?"

SOME PEOPLE AREN'T MEANT TO BE SAVED

"Well, he rang here early. Like really early. It was about 8.30am. I thought something was up at first, he sounded desperate to get hold of you. Obviously, I was limited to what I could tell him, but I ended up telling him you and Ellie we're still asleep, which brought me some time but not much. He's rang 3 times today and honestly Al, I ran out of excuses"

"So, what did you tell him, Lee? Did you tell him where I was, what?"

"You're freaking me out now. How do you want me to handle the situation when you give me no insight Alice? Maybe you wouldn't need to be so abrupt if you tried answering your phone"

"Have you told him yes, or no?"

"No! But I did tell him you don't want to speak to him right now. I got tired of lying for you a long time ago Alice".

I hung up immediately.

I was so pissed off. Why is it that I am always the burden? The hindrance. The liability. Why do I always feel like the one in the firing line? And why does everything always decide to happen all in one go? At this point, it really was just a case of sink or swim.

Lisa was ringing again. I really was not in the mood.

"Alice, you better think of something quick, I've got Ed on the housephone?"

I had an idea. It probably wasn't going to work but I wasn't sure what else to do.

"Lisa is there any way you can turn the volume up on the house phone?"

SOME PEOPLE AREN'T MEANT TO BE SAVED

"What?" asked Lisa. She sounded annoyed.
"Like so I can hear him?"
"Yes, I know what you mean, I just don't get why you're asking"
"Put us both on speaker phone and leave the phones next to each other", I said.
I can't risk letting him know I'm not with Lisa. I have to convince him.
If not. He will show up here.
He'd have to find me first but he's a stubborn bastard.
I wish he were just as determined to move and heaven hell for the other things in his life.
I could hear Lee walking from room to room and letting Ed know she was passing the phone over.
I felt sick not knowing if this was going to work but I had no option but to roll with it.
"Avoiding my calls, is that how this is going to work from now on?" asked Ed.
I could picture his face.
"Ed now isn't the time. I said what I needed to and it's not like…", he cut me off.
"Like what? Like you've abducted our daughter and done a disappearing act?", he followed.
"Abducted? Ed, I've come to Lee's for a few days. I thought after what happened we could just both do with some space. Please…"
"Apart from the fact you only told me after you'd left? I had no fucking say Alice! None at all" Ed said aggressively.
"Ed…" He interrupted again.

SOME PEOPLE AREN'T MEANT TO BE SAVED

"Don't Ed me, I want Ellie fucking home now. We'll talk about it when you get here" he demanded.
He was clearly still angry. I very much doubted things were going to be okay.
"I'm staying for two weeks, Ed. I don't think coming back while things are so tense is good for either of us. You, me, Ellie. Surely you agree?"
I don't know where that came from.
I didn't even want to stay two weeks. I hadn't thought about it before this conversation either, I swear.
I think I just felt pressured in the moment and struggled to see a way out. It just slipped out.
It was too late to take it back now.
He was laughing. That just made me feel even worse, but it didn't last long.
"If you think you're upping sticks and taking Ellie away from me Alice, I promise you, you'll come to regret it you bitch!"
I choked up trying not to cry.
My mouth felt dry, and I just wanted to curl up into a ball.
I had no intentions to take Ellie.
The thought of Lisa being able to hear every word said just made me want to clam up and without thinking I just hung up.
I let half an hour pass by without even moving.
I just stayed slumped in the kitchen. I couldn't bring myself to move, I just wanted to die at that moment to be honest.
The guilt always sets in though when I think of Ellie.
I feel selfish for having terrible thoughts.

SOME PEOPLE AREN'T MEANT TO BE SAVED

How could I possibly think about doing anything like that when I had that precious little girl by my side.
Things aren't always so black and white though. It's not that she's not enough to stop me having the thoughts I do. Sometimes I convince myself that even she would be better off without me, it's weird.
I snap out of it though. It just gets tough sometimes.
I don't usually like sharing that with people and I know why too.
'Attention seeker'.
I hate that fucking label.
Of course, we're fucking attention seeking. Of course, we want someone to stop us. Of course, we want to feel more than the emotions we do in that moment. Why is that so extraordinary to people? Why do we even have to put a label on such a sensitive moment?
I think I'm starting to realise for the first time that I'm not angry at just one thing.
I'm angry at the world.
I'm angry for reasons I'm only just starting to understand fully.
Maybe that's the reason I'm so frustrated? We're so obsessed with labels that we're too quick to assume our problems have only one cause and thus, one answer.
Life is so much more complicated than that.
I wish someone understood what I was trying to say or could fill in the bits I'm missing.
I just remembered I hadn't spoken with Lisa about the whole 'staying for another two weeks' thing.

SOME PEOPLE AREN'T MEANT TO BE SAVED

She's going to have something to say about that.
And I was right.
She did.
I checked my phone to see a text from Lee asking me to call her when I had the chance.
Is it just me that thinks that's weird?
She's been so… abrupt the past couple of times we have spoken. The text sounded softer, like she was trying to speak to me differently.
Like she was trying.
After not seeing one another for a while, the idea of rebuilding our relationship felt good.
I love Ellie, but sometimes it's nice to be in the company of other adults sometimes.
Curiosity was getting the better of me. I picked the phone up and decided I was going to call her.
No stalling.
She didn't answer.
Strange.
I thought about ringing again, but I was feeling a little anxious. I locked my phone and put it down when Lisa's name popped up on my phone.
"Hey Alice, how are you? How's Ellie?", she said softly. I really was confused now.
"Well Ellie's asleep but she's had a good day and I'm okay. You?" I wasn't sure how else to reply.
"Are you sure you're, okay? There isn't anything you aren't telling me is there?" she asked.
I knew something seemed off.

SOME PEOPLE AREN'T MEANT TO BE SAVED

"Of course, I'm, okay? Is this about the call before because I was going to explain?" I started thinking she was getting suspicious of Ed. That last part was quite bitter.
"Actually Alice, I spoke with Ed after and…"
I interrupted, "you and Ed? When?"
"When you hung up, what else could I have done? I had to tell him you left the room, he was pissed the fuck off Alice", she said.
I didn't even think about that.
I was feeling sick with the thought that hanging up might have given the game away.
I'm sure the phone makes a tone when it disconnects?
I fucked it.
"He knows I'm not with you, doesn't he?"
"He didn't mention anything actually but come to think of it, I'm lying on your behalf and even I don't know where the hell you are, Alice. Ed said he's worried about your mental state or something and that you haven't been taking your tablets? And he definitely sounded like he shouldn't have been mentioning the tablets. What are you hiding Al? Are you sick?"
She sounded like she had more questions where they came from, but I had to cut in and put a stop to it.
What the fuck was going on?
"No! Of course, I'm not ill. Listen Lee, things have just been a bit tense at home lately and I could do with some space. Why do I feel like I'm being interrogated?" I asked her.
"Because you don't speak to any of your family or friends anymore Alice and you're staying in some random location

and taking Ellie without even telling Ed! You've got to admit things sound sort of off?"

"Well thanks for taking the opportunity to remind me I'm surrounded by absolutely no one and why can't I just be staying in a hotel? Why do you assume I'm staying in some random location?"

I know I was lying but it's not like I step out of line often. I just wanted some peace and quiet.

I feel suffocated most days.

"Because you took no money with you Al, and another thing…"

"How do you know I have nothing on me? Only Ed could have told you that. Just exactly what has he said, Lee?"

I feel impatient now. Nothing was making sense.

"Nothing bad. He sounded more worried than anything. He said he was worried about you and that you were in no fit state to be taking Ellie anywhere, especially now you aren't on your medication. Obviously, I reassured him about the money thing but then he thanked me for saving your arse with the house or something? He said you've been behaving out of character lately and just urged me to get you home as soon as possible. Please just tell me what's going on Alice, can I help you get Ellie home?" she said desperately.

Wow.

She thought I was fucking insane.

What was Ed playing at? What right did he have to start shouting my business off like I was some sort of mad woman? The self-doubt started kicking in, of course it did.

"Lee, if I promise to meet you soon, will you please respect

the time I need right now and believe in me when I say everything is under control?" I didn't have the energy to convince her about anything, I was feeling too betrayed by Ed.
"Tomorrow?", she said eagerly.
"I don't really know about tomorrow Lee…"
"It's tomorrow Alice or I'm not covering for you anymore. Your choice?"
I agreed.
I told her I'd text her with a time and location tomorrow then wrapped the call up.
I didn't want to go but I didn't want an argument again. Or to be made to feel like my feelings weren't worth acknowledging again.
As I came off the phone, I noticed Ed had sent a text. I was surprised to see he had only sent one, but it was enough to send shivers through my body.
It was just one word.
Nothing else.
'Home', it said.
It's late now.
I don't even feel tired. It's like I wake up more at night.
I think it's because it's the only time in the day I can just think without interruption. My thoughts are my own worst enemy, which is why I try to understand them.
Maybe if I could get to know them more, I could remember how to be happy again. I was still confused about the things Ed said to Lisa.
I haven't mentioned this yet, but I was diagnosed with manic

depression a few years ago.
I never had any previous encounters with this illness before.
I don't really talk a lot about it.
It isn't exactly a conversational topic.
Another life struggle that ordinary people just see as an act of 'attention seeking'.
I was one of those ignorant people before my first encounter too.
I didn't really understand it.
In fact, I've only started to understand it that little better since speaking with Pete.
It's crazy how you move when you learn to understand things better.
I'm not building you up to an excuse for coming off my medication, honestly. If I'm honest, I still can't fathom why Ed had the nerve to bring up my medication. He was always telling me I didn't need them and to sort my head out. Then again, he used to taunt me and call me a crazy bitch too whenever he wanted to use me as a verbal punching bag.
I got tired of trying to wipe the mud he left on my name, time and time again.
It was easier to put up and shut up.
Maybe that's why I am always so torn about whether I identify as crazy or not? Because he's fucking confused me with his contradictive bullshit.
Argh!
Writing this all down tonight has been a bit of a release. Nothing quite like having someone to talk to but I guess I'll

SOME PEOPLE AREN'T MEANT TO BE SAVED

have to make do.
Time for another restless night.

SOME PEOPLE AREN'T MEANT TO BE SAVED

ONE STEP AT A TIME

Ed has sent countless texts as you probably expected. I tried my best to not let it bother me as much as it had been.
If this time away was going to count for anything then I had to use it wisely.
I left to get away from treading on eggshells. I
t took me a couple of hours to realise I promised Lisa that Ellie and I would meet her today. Part of me thought I might be able to play it off like I forgot about it to avoid going, but she texted me at 11am asking if I had a location and time in mind yet. See what I mean? No escaping.
I was screaming inside, rolling my eyes on the outside.
I hadn't mentioned anything to Ellie yet. I knew she would get excited if I did and I didn't want to let her down if I couldn't bring myself to go.
I think I was just anxious about the questions that were bound to fly in my direction. I think it felt worse because of

SOME PEOPLE AREN'T MEANT TO BE SAVED

the length of time we had gone without seeing each other. They say absence makes the heart grow fonder, but I don't think it applies in our situation.
Ed's texts were getting more aggressive by the minute.
I thought about blocking his number, but I couldn't do it. Imagine the things he'd be saying then.
I'm going to have to sort something out for Ellie and her dad. It isn't fair that either of them misses out because I need some space.
There was another side of me though that kept questioning Ellie's safety in Ed's company.
Thinking that out loud sounds crazy.
Probably as crazy as writing 'thinking out loud'.
Back on topic though, watching from a distance has really helped me to see how much Ed and I are struggling and the ways in which things are only worsening with time.
If time is such a great healer, why aren't things getting better?
We've been in a mess for four years now and I really don't want to give up, but I feel like I already have.
I stopped loving him a long time ago and he doesn't think twice before laying his hands on me anymore.
I honestly don't recognise him.
His personality was starting to outshine his physical looks and the Ed that I knew disappeared the longer he'd been on that shit.
Thing is he was amazing when we first met, so I know he's a good man deep down.
I don't like to blame him.

SOME PEOPLE AREN'T MEANT TO BE SAVED

Although, I think over time, that has bit me in the arse.
It's like it's made him believe he has no control over things completely. He blames everything but himself now.
I've done that.
I didn't even realise the damage it was doing but it was physically re-writing the way he looked at justifying his actions.
I told him it wasn't his fault over and over again, with no acknowledgment for the things he was accountable for, until eventually we both believed it.
I feel like I shouldn't be writing all this down.
It's a lot for a person you know nothing about.
I just want you to understand the full picture for all the ugly that it is.
Maybe that way, you can make sense of it from all angles.
I don't want to believe he would hurt Ellie, but I'd be a rubbish Mum to disregard it.
I can tell he's struggling to keep his cool around her lately too.
I want to believe he wants to change but he makes it so fucking hard.
The thought of abandoning him when he needs me the most makes me sick to my stomach.
But the more I think about it I realise he left me to deal with my troubles alone a long time ago.
Two wrongs don't make a right though, as they say.
Although that's another expression that doesn't make sense when you apply it to reality.
Just take a look at the justice system for example.

SOME PEOPLE AREN'T MEANT TO BE SAVED

A very fluent example of the eye for an eye metaphor if you look closely.
The world works in contradictory ways.
It depends on labels and definitions.
So, consumed by wrong and right that everything else gets lost in between.
Maybe going to see Lisa wouldn't be a bad thing.
It would stop me sloping off into my own world. I have a headache from all the thinking I've done over the past few days.
Ellie would enjoy meeting her aunty properly. They've met before but Ellie was really young. Lee has a little boy now too. I haven't met him yet.
I wonder if she will bring him.
I better not mention anything to Ellie just in case.
I text Lisa and arranged to meet at a cute coffee location closer to her.
I know she liked coffee, maybe a bit of thought might soften the initial blow.
I was so nervous as we headed to see her.
I wanted to get there before her.
I picked a table outdoors; it was a nice day and seemed a bit more private too.
I didn't want our conversation bouncing off the walls into the ears of others.
I still wasn't sure how it was going to go.
Ellie loved sitting on the cute chairs.
She was excited to meet her aunty, Lisa.
I ordered Ellie some food and a milkshake when I saw Lisa

getting out of the taxi, on her own.
I was a bit disappointed, but I totally get why she chose not to bring him.
She didn't know what to expect either and I haven't exactly given her a lot to go off.
As she sat down, we sort of awkwardly exchanged hellos and made the effort to half smile. It was more than I expected. Probably more than we both expected.
I found myself speaking more to Ellie than Lisa at first.
I think she could tell I was trying to avoid talking to her. Not in the way that it sounds.
I was just nervous.
I think part of her was thankful for it too.
It was our way of breaking the ice.
"She looks like you", said Lisa.
"You think?" I said smiling.
"Yeah. The you I knew when I last saw you" she followed.
I didn't know how to respond to that, so I let the silence take over.
"You look… different Alice. Are you eating, okay?" said Lisa.
She actually sounded concerned.
"You never did have a filter, did you?" I said giggling.
She giggled and said, "what, and you did?"
She started laughing too.
"I've just lost my appetite the older I've got, it's nothing to worry about", I said, gesturing my head towards Ellie.
I wasn't sure if talking about this in front of Ellie was the wisest idea.

SOME PEOPLE AREN'T MEANT TO BE SAVED

"Do you have any earphones, Lee?"
"Let me check my bag, hold on a sec… Here you go."
I passed Ellie them with my phone and helped her put a film on Netflix.
She was in her element.
Oh, the joys of being a child. I wish I hadn't wished the time away growing up now.
"Al, this shit can't be filtered. You look worn out babe. I don't want to stress you out any more than you may be but I'm worried. Like I haven't seen you for years and now all of a sudden, we're here, you're avoiding Ed, you've been on medication and I'm lying for you. You've got to help me understand things here because from where I'm sitting, you're expecting me to carry the weight of a burden I know nothing about," said Lisa.
It was deeper than I expected for the first point of contact and definitely less angry than I expected her to be too.
"It's so much more complicated than you'll know and by the sounds of it, you've already made your mind up" I replied.
I didn't come prepared for a heart to heart so I wanted to avoid one where possible.
I'm not sad so I don't need anyone else's pity.
"You haven't even given me the chance," she said.
I suppose she was right there, but you try explaining a problem you haven't even figured out yourself yet.
"Can we do that thing Mum used to teach us about whenever we disagreed?" I asked.
"The thing where we try to absorb one another's perspective?" Lisa giggled.

SOME PEOPLE AREN'T MEANT TO BE SAVED

"That's the one. The 'technique' she learnt on that course that time, do you remember?" I followed.
We were both laughing at this point.
It had been a long time since I'd laughed in the company of another adult. It took me back to old times for a minute.
It felt empowering until I realised we had to return to talking about more serious shit.
"Well, if I'm being honest things are hard to talk about at the moment. They don't really make sense fully in my own head yet and trying to carry it all and raise Ellie is so... testing sometimes. I want so badly to give her the life me and Ed planned but..."
I couldn't find the words to follow, and I was trying not to speak ill of Ed.
"But?" she asked.
She was doing that thing when just one side of her face raises as she tries to piece things together in her head as she waits.
"I don't know how to shorten it. I'm trying but there's so much that's happened since things went sour between us.
I regretted calling because I knew how much pressure I'd be putting on you and if I honestly had any other option, I would have taken it" I said with sorrow.
"We still haven't talked about Mum Al. Where were you when she died? The funeral? It's like you just went completely off radar and to look at you now... It's like looking at a different person. What's going on with this medication and what is it for?" she asked.
There were a lot of questions and each of them overwhelmed me for different reasons.

SOME PEOPLE AREN'T MEANT TO BE SAVED

I knew I had all the answers she was looking for, but some I was still discovering, and the rest seemed to be unretrievable.
"I know you have a lot of questions and I want to answer them, it's just… a lot of history in a short time. What if we start talking and the bits I tell you don't convince you enough that I'm not this bitch you paint me to be in your head. I have reasons but that doesn't mean they'll make sense to you. Then what?" I asked.
"Then we take that shit as it comes but if we don't start somewhere, we're all going to be bouncing around and playing our individual roles in feeding a negative situation, fuel. It just depends on if you're ready to be the break or the explosion. From where I sit, you don't seem to have a lot of options?" she stated.
It felt like she reaffirmed thoughts I'd been having over the last couple of days and for the first time in a long time, I didn't feel crazy.
I feel better when someone validates my thoughts, it's like my anxiety turns its back on me for a minute or two.
"Things aren't as black and white as they appear, you know me. I love Mum. I love you. I know you think about the things I did or didn't do and feel saddened by it, but it hurt me not to be there. Things had been off for a while before Mum died but I feel like no one cared enough to ask or turned a blind eye to vital signs that could have made a difference between life and… this" I said. I choked up.
I think I actually lost breath before reaching the end of my sentence.

SOME PEOPLE AREN'T MEANT TO BE SAVED

My mouth was moving but no sound was coming out.
Lisa hung her head. I'm not sure she knew what to say.
I don't blame her. As humans we often try to make things better where necessary, and we feel a sense of guilt if we feel like we are unable to achieve that.
It doesn't matter what context you apply that thesis to.
I didn't mind that she couldn't find the words to say.
If anything, it was refreshing.
I didn't want solutions or answers, I wanted for one minute to not feel like I was overreacting.
Like for one moment, my problem warranted my disorientation. To feel normal and not crazy.
"Hello Daddy" we heard Ellie say.
Our heads lifted.
I could see Ed's name on the screen.
I didn't even think when I gave her the phone.
I couldn't just rip it off her, I didn't want to scare her.
We stayed quiet to try and listen to what was being said, but with the earphones in, it was hard to hear a word of what Ed was saying to Ellie.
"Yeah Daddy, we're at the tea shop at the moment, it's really cool. We're sitting outside" she said.
I couldn't stop thinking about what he was asking her.
I wasn't as worried as I would have been if this had happened when I was on my own.
At least I was with Lisa. It would work in my favour in getting to believe I was with her.
I tried to act as cool as possible to avoid any more questions than necessary.

SOME PEOPLE AREN'T MEANT TO BE SAVED

I thought it might be a good idea if Ed could hear mine and Lisa's voice in the background.
"I can't believe how big Oscar's getting, Lee. Can you send me those photos of the kids?" I said to Lisa with wide eyes, hoping she would catch my drift. She looked at me confused so I nodded my head to hurry her on.
"There's loads you know; do you want me to send them all in one go?" Lisa asked. I love the way she plays the part for me so well.
"Send a few at a time when Ellie comes off the phone" I replied.
I thought saying that might prompt the conversation to end but things took a turn.
Ellie only went and slipped up about the 'holiday home'.
My stomach dropped, if he hadn't shown his true potential before, this was sure going to provoke him.
I know it's not her fault, she's just a kid but bloody hell.
Just when things couldn't get any worse.
This is why I get overwhelmed because every time I try to start ciphering through my problems one at a time, something pops up in another area of my life and before you know it, I'm making rash decisions and pissing people off. When is it going to stop?
I think these days have dragged more than they would if I were at home. For different reasons that obviously wouldn't make sense to you.
I had zoned out, but I could see Ellie holding the phone in my direction out of the corner of my eye.
I took the phone from her hand.

SOME PEOPLE AREN'T MEANT TO BE SAVED

I could hear him effing and jeffing before I even placed it to my ear.
I tried to turn the volume down in a hurry.
I was so embarrassed.
What was Lisa going to think?
I wasn't even listening to Ed; I was too busy looking at everyone walking by.
I just felt like everyone could hear what was going on. I know they couldn't, but it didn't stop me worrying about it.
I lost it.
"Fuck sake Ed, why don't you fuck listen. Of course, it's like a holiday for Ellie, stop twisting her words and give me some space. The sooner you give us space, the sooner we'll be able to talk like adults and without this continuous tension".
"Don't you dare speak to me like that. I can imagine you now, sat there playing the victim to anyone that will listen, villainising me and getting away with the bullshit fact that you've ran off with our fucking child to fuck knows where. Now I'm telling you once and once only, Alice, so listen up and pay fucking close attention…" he started.
He sounded so calm.
I tried to look up to avoid the buildup of tears in my eyes falling on my cheeks.
"I'll give you some time but if you don't have Ellie back here where she belongs in a matter of days, I'll make sure you never see her again and I mean that Alice. And if you aren't where you say you are either and I find out, I'll do an even better job of making sure you don't find us either. Now make of that what you will but I am not fucking about. I'm tired of

SOME PEOPLE AREN'T MEANT TO BE SAVED

your hormonal bullshit".
He hung up the phone, but I still kept it to my ear in the hopes that Lisa wouldn't start questioning me straight away.
A couple of girls from the table across were looking over and whispering.
I felt so embarrassed, but I just wanted everything to stop. What a way of not drawing attention to myself.
I chose to believe that Ed meant what he said about at least giving me a few days but in the back of my mind I knew he would probably disrupt it in some way.
"Alice, whatever is going on you know you can talk to me, right?" Lisa asked.
Here comes the sympathy.
I didn't want to talk.
I'll talk when I'm ready but right now the only thing I crave is normality.
Luckily, Lisa was on the ball and managed to make sure that Ellie heard nothing by letting her use her phone while I was on mine to Ed.
"I do, and I don't. Don't take that the wrong way. I know I can talk to you but I'm so worried about the judgments you'll pass and the things you'll keep to yourself. I'm struggling like fuck right now and I honestly see no way out no matter which way I look. Ed is going through a lot of shit. Like, a lot. It's put a massive strain on our relationship, and everything has changed. I feel bad about Mum, about you, about everything. I know you all think I just cut ties. I wish you would have tried to dig deeper. Don't get me wrong I'm not saying any of this is on you because it isn't. I accept the

SOME PEOPLE AREN'T MEANT TO BE SAVED

part I played but a lot more has been going on beneath the surface. I've tried to cope with my diagnosis on my own because I got fed up with tiring myself out trying to understand it just to be able to explain it to everyone else. I avoid social situations so that I don't have to hear from everyone else about how much I've changed or weight I've lost or gained. I realise all these things before anyone else does. You didn't know Ed cheated or took drugs. And even now you'll never know just what lengths I've gone to not make shit about me. I just need someone to cut me some slack".

I was surprised I held my nerve.

I said more than I thought I would, but the worst bit was not being able to predict how she was going to interpret it all.

I felt guilty. Like I was overpowering her version of events. They weren't my intentions but for the first time ever I wanted to try being honest no matter who my truth upset.

I just wanted to be heard.

"Jesus, Alice. I mean, I don't even know which bit to get stuck in first. I can't believe I've been none the wiser that you've been coping with all of this on your own… Drugs? I don't get where Ed's version comes into it though? Why is he making you out to be the mad one and how long has this been going on for?" Lisa asked in awe.

I felt like she didn't believe me.

Maybe I shouldn't have laid it out thick like that right away. It was already out now though.

"The drugs have always been an on and off pleasure of Ed's. He always promised he had control over it and that they didn't control him and naively, I believed him. Why wouldn't I? I thought it was just something he did on a night out. But nights out became more frequent. Then he lost his job. We argue all the time. To be honest it feels weird when we don't..." I spoke.

"I know this is a sensitive question, but has he ever hit you? You just seem more tense than I remember? And something doesn't make sense, it's like you're scared of him?" Lisa asked upfront.

I clammed up.

She just wouldn't get it.

Things have been physically tense for a while, but it's not something I was ready to think about.

"Sorry, maybe that was a bit more forward than intended. Today's been a bit of a day, why don't you both come back to ours for pizza?" Lisa suggested.

She knows it's my favourite.

I wanted to but something was holding me back.

"That sounds amazing, and I'd hate to be a party pooper, but I've got some thinking to do. What about if we do this again though? Soon?" I asked.

"I'd love that. I'll ring us a taxi now and maybe I could give you a ring later?"

"Thanks Lee" I smiled.

Ellie wasn't happy that we were leaving but she perked up when I mentioned when I would be seeing Lee again soon.

I regretted making these promises not long after.

I felt like I'd lined up another afternoon of anxiety.

I was just hoping it would get easier.

SOME PEOPLE AREN'T MEANT TO BE SAVED

I enjoyed seeing my sister today.
It went better than I expected too and although it was hard, I was finally starting to feel like I was benefiting from the time away.
I started repairing old bonds and it was nice to get another perspective.
Ellie's asleep now so I'm sitting on the floor of the bathroom crying and writing and trying to wrap my head around the realms of emotions I'd experienced today and the fears I managed to overcome independently.
There was still a lot for me and Lee to go over and talk about but for now I was simply happy to be back in her life.
I hadn't heard from Ed since, which was a good sign and Lee forgot to call this evening too. I won't lie, I'm sort of grateful.
My eyes are puffy, I think it's time to hit the sheets.
I hope this is the start of something better.
I don't think I can cope with stress.

SOME PEOPLE AREN'T MEANT TO BE SAVED

THE THINGS YOU CAN'T CHANGE

I didn't go straight to sleep last night. I stayed up thinking about ways that I could start my day better. I felt clearer minded knowing that Ed was going to allow us to have the space we needed and thought I should put it to some use. It still felt strange though.

I couldn't help but think about the card the driver gave me on the way here.

A part of me was considering going. I didn't want to talk about my problems, but I thought it might do me some good to be around people that understand me more than the people around me.

I know that sounds ungrateful and I don't mean it too.

It's just I've been learning that one of my biggest problems is not feeling understood.

Maybe if I could listen to the perspectives of those who

experienced similar things to me, I may be able to piece things together in an orderly sense.

I tried to look for the card to see if I could find the number, but I couldn't remember if I'd thrown it away or just placed it out of sight.

Eventually I found it and I won't go into too much depth, but I rang them after some time to enquire about drop-in availability.

I spoke with Gill who reassured me I am able to drop-in whenever I like. They had a creche there for children which I thought was amazing.

There wasn't really anything standing in my way now childcare wasn't a problem.

It couldn't do any harm to attend could it?

A part of me was anxious at the thought of leaving Ellie in a room on her own, in a building we hadn't been to before and with people we didn't know.

I was worried about whether the environment was appropriate, but she seemed happy to go. She thought it was going to be a drop and play sort of experience.

I packed her a goody bag to take with her in incase she felt peck-ish. I thought it might make the experience a little better for her.

I was just trying to make the best out of a bad situation really. I didn't have any alternatives and if I don't sort myself out soon, I'm honestly scared I'll end up a lost cause.

I feel myself slipping away with each passing day.

I already struggle to remember the me I used to be.

What if I lose that forever?

SOME PEOPLE AREN'T MEANT TO BE SAVED

When we got there, I wanted to turn back.
We stood outside the front while I lit up a cigarette.
I haven't smoked in years but figured I could do with some form of stress relief.
Cigs make it easier for me to slope off for two undenied minutes of escapism.
The building looked quite run down.
It wasn't so bad inside, and I could tell the creche had recently been assembled together. I thought it was lovely that the group catered for people with children.
I wasn't sure if other places were the same. This was the first time I'd been to something like this – a lot of it is hard to access.
I was in a mental health support group but that was online. I didn't actually have to speak to people.
My nerves started kicking in as I walked up to the desk to ask for direction. A lady took us through to the creche to get Ellie settled.
She ran straight in without a second thought. I wish I had her confidence.
It was silent as we walked to the room the session was being held in, which I didn't mind.
It was a small group. There must have only been about ten of us in the room.
Men and women.
I could feel everyone looking at me, so I tried to concentrate on getting to a seat and sitting down.
The lady that managed the group was called Gill - she must have been the driver's wife.

SOME PEOPLE AREN'T MEANT TO BE SAVED

She didn't look like I'd imagined her too.
I think I was lost in staring at her when she said, "It's nice to have you here with us today…"
"Hope!" I jumped in.
I tried to smile.
I'm not sure if it looked that way but at least I tried.
It made me feel better to be here as someone else.
I hoped I was going to be asked to speak about anything right away.
I was sweating which probably makes no sense since it wasn't warm in the building.
I think it was nerves.
I kept fidgeting too.
The chairs weren't the comfiest.
I tried to stay focused on keeping still as I wasn't sure if I was distracting the people at either side of me.
I tuned into my surroundings eventually.
One of the women was sharing her story. I didn't really know where to put myself as she spoke of how bad her previous relationship had been.
You could still see faint bruises on her arms and face. In fact, the longer I sat looking around the room, the more I realised I didn't deserve to be here at all. My story was nowhere near as bad as everyone else's. I wasn't sitting here with cuts and bruises - well not visible ones anyway. I didn't have the same stories. I wasn't feeling scared. I wasn't crying.
In fact, I just felt numb.
It felt wrong to be here.
I couldn't do it.

SOME PEOPLE AREN'T MEANT TO BE SAVED

"I'm sorry, I can't do this", I said as I ran out the door.
I didn't stop running.
I don't even know how long I was running for, but I know it took me a while to slow down.
I think I was lost at the moment.
I just wanted to get away.
I wasn't thinking about much more.
I slowed as I saw a taxi approaching the sidewalk a little further down the road. I jumped in and asked him to drive.
I wasn't sure where I was going, and the driver seemed really confused too but we went with it.
All I could think about was my mum. I wanted nothing more than for her to be here now. I needed her to tell me what to do and how to fix the mess that was my life. It felt like I was losing a grip on reality.
I asked the driver to take me to her grave. It wasn't the same as sitting with her face to face, but I didn't really know what else to do.
It was the first time I'd been to see my mum's grave since she died four years ago.
You probably think I'm a bitch, but things were hard.
I wanted to come and see her but the longer I left it, the worse I felt. I figured if I could bring myself to see Lisa yesterday, I could definitely pluck the courage to stand by Mum's grave.
I could see her headstone, so I headed towards it.
The closer I got, the more relieved I was starting to feel, it was weird.
I sat on the grass next to her and started talking.

SOME PEOPLE AREN'T MEANT TO BE SAVED

"Hi mum. It's me, Alice. I'm sorry I haven't been to see you. In fact, I'm sorry for a lot of things. I feel ashamed to only be sitting here now but things have been hard Mum. I wish you were here to tell me what to do, stroke my face and tell me everything is going to be okay. I don't really know where to start with it all, it's such a mess Mum. Things aren't working out between me and Ed and they haven't been since you died. I blamed him for a lot of things which was probably unfair, but I was so angry when you died. I know you probably hate me for not being there as you got worse. I wouldn't blame you. I hate myself. I know you won't believe this, but I wanted so badly to be with you as you got worse. I didn't want to move. Ed wanted to be closer to his family, not that we see any of them ever. Ellie's lucky to get a card for her birthday and Ed? He never hears off his Mum. His Dad is still wrapped up in his own little fantasy world and Ed's not far behind. I'm worried about him Mum. I don't recognise him. It was hard to talk to you when you were ill. I didn't want you to worry about whether or not I could take care of myself when you'd gone. I wanted you to be confident that I could take care of shit and I've tried".

I paused for a moment while another family passed by.

I didn't want them to hear what I was saying.

"You're probably wondering why I haven't mentioned the funeral yet. I think that's because that's where everything started. It's hard to talk about so it's gotten easier to avoid as time has passed. I remember Ellie's first birthday like it was yesterday. I was so excited our baby was turning one, but I remember how poorly you were. You'd gone into the hospice by this point and Ed's behaviour was getting worse. He started taking drugs more frequently and lashing out when he didn't have them. Money was like water to him; we were struggling to make it stretch every single month. It got to the point where some months we were relying on the food bank but even then, that was hit and miss on the months our income was considered too high. I thought he'd lost sight of reality then but he's worse now. We argued on the night of Ellie's birthday while she was asleep. I asked for some money so that I could come up to see you but of course it was an issue. We argued for hours. Things got a bit nasty on both sides. I was just so angry. I hadn't seen you much since we moved and not being able to look after you after you was heartbreaking", I felt myself choke up again.

"Then I got the call from Lee to say you'd died a few days later and my world just shattered into a million pieces. That was it, I was never going to see you again and I was beating myself up about what you must have thought as you laid there weak and fragile."

I started crying by this point.

I still got the same feeling every time I thought of or talked about Mum's last days. In fact, the feeling intensified the more time passed.

"I couldn't have come to the funeral in the state I was in. I knew everyone would be looking at me like the bad apple of the family, almost like I had no right to be there. When you died... I was a wreck. Me and Ed were arguing more by the day, he showed no sympathy whatsoever. It was like he was dead inside, Mum. honestly. I was either beating myself

about you or for pissing Ed off in some way. My head was all over the place. When you died, I blamed him for everything. I told him how depressing my life had been since moving. How I blamed him for never getting to say goodbye. It angered him. A lot more than necessary. It confused me that he wasn't upset to hear what I was saying. That's when I knew something was wrong. He told me how ungrateful I was. That he was sick and tired of me moaning. He was getting louder and louder. Screaming in my face. I try not to think about what happened after that often. Long story short, I was black and blue. How could I come to a funeral like that? And how was I supposed to tell you all this with everything you had going on, Mum, how? I just couldn't. I felt stuck. Like I had no one to talk to. That's the day I fell out of love with Ed. And then every day after that as I looked at myself in the mirror each day. I just... resented him. I don't think I've realised that up until now, but it makes perfect sense."
I paused to wipe my nose.
I felt all bunged up and emotional but in a weird way lighter. Free-er.
Is that even a word?
I still hadn't got everything off my chest, but it did help me reflect on some of the deeper issues I've been ignoring for some time.
Although my mind has been a tough place to be lost in over these last few days, things were starting to make sense.
"Shit!"
How am I sitting here?

SOME PEOPLE AREN'T MEANT TO BE SAVED

Ellie!
I'd left her at the group creche.
I threw up.
I was struggling to think straight, stay focused. My heart was palpitating.
Luckily, I had some water in my bag.
I couldn't find my phone. I'd looked in every pocket and section, but it was nowhere.
I can't have lost it. I haven't used it since arriving at the group, had I?
Argh! I can't think straight.
I got up, took a deep breath and looked at Mum's headstone.
What would you do Mum? I thought.
I blew her a kiss and with tears in my eyes I walked off.
I started picking up pace. I was trying to focus and think straight but the more I tried, the harder I was finding it.
I looked at the time and felt scared.
The group session usually runs for about an hour, I think. I've been gone for two.
I didn't even know if the creche would still be open.
What if she'd wandered off? What if they called the police? They will have definitely assumed I wasn't in a stable state upon leaving. What if they've called social services?
I can't believe I just left her.
I'm not trying to stick up for myself, but things are so heavy at the moment. I know how slack that sounds. That's not something I would usually do, I swear.
I started feeling sicker and sicker, so I reached in my bag for my water and there was my phone.

SOME PEOPLE AREN'T MEANT TO BE SAVED

I was so confused.
It wasn't there before.
Or maybe it was and I'm going crazy?
I really can't keep up.
I was more bothered about getting hold of a taxi.
I was imagining all the possible worst-case scenarios that could have happened.
I was thinking about what I could say that would justify my actions. Not because I didn't recognise the error of my ways but because I just needed someone; anyone, to understand me. Was that so awful?
I don't want to lose my little girl, but I just know they're going to think I'm an awful Mum.
No one in those roles actually cares.
It's just a job to them. A pay cheque.
I shouldn't say no one but it just feels like it.
I can't stress just how dismissive my GP is where it comes to my mental health. In fact, I've never been able to get past the prick to even speak to someone who actually specialises in what they're talking about. Instead, I have to put up with his uneducated remarks, offensive 'depression score' questionnaires and fobbed off with a priced prescription.
I mean it really says it all when you realise you live in a world that makes you pay for good health.
I should have stayed home.
Better the devil you know.
Instead, I'm in a taxi to find out if my daughter is in the same place, I left her when I fucked off without a care in the world.
I was torn between feeling selfish and easy going on myself.

SOME PEOPLE AREN'T MEANT TO BE SAVED

I think I snapped like that because I never get a moment to myself.
Not to think.
Not to grieve.
But how do we know whose fault it is when we exhibit behaviours out of the ordinary? Who's to blame right now? Is it me? Or was I bound to explode?
I can't remember the last time I didn't overthink things.
My head was starting to hurt again.
As we pulled up, I was a mess. I almost forgot to pay the driver.
I ran through, past the main reception and into the creche. I was trying to tell Ellie apart from the other kids. I scanned the room twice, but I couldn't see her.
Everyone stared at me as I ran through, checking every space in the room but she just wasn't there.
Where was she? I could hear the staff in the background but the noise in my head was drowning them out.
Gill came to the reception and raced toward me in a hurry.
"Hope!" I could hear her shouting.
I was confused for a second until I remembered I'd used a fake name.
She sat beside me and sighed. I couldn't work out if she was disappointed or relieved but I'm sure I was going to find out, so I rolled with the moment.
"Just tell me?" I said hopelessly.
I looked at her with tears in my eyes. Part of me was hoping she was going to cut me a break and put me out of my misery. I just wanted to know where my little girl was.

SOME PEOPLE AREN'T MEANT TO BE SAVED

A couple of the staff from reception were peering over.
I felt so anxious.
"Hope. Little Ellie is fine. I thought I'd just give you a moment to ground yourself. Do you think you might be ready to talk? Or would you like some more time?" said Gill.
"Can I see her please?" I asked desperately.
"Of course, you can. You're her mother. My advice would be to have a moment and a chat though? You'll be surprised how much you might appreciate another voice to listen to at the moment" Gill replied.
All of a sudden, I didn't feel as anxious, but she could just be doing her job and calming me down.
I couldn't be sure yet, but it couldn't do any harm to talk. I have been avoiding it.
Maybe I'm afraid of what I'll hear.
I don't know.
"I appreciate you being so calm and understanding. I think I would like that, but will Ellie be, okay? I still don't know what she's doing?"
"She's in our second creche room with some of the other kids. We thought she might have enjoyed it more in the other room. They were doing some artsy stuff and she got overly excited when she found out, I hope that is okay?" Gill responded.
I smiled a little.
She was such a creative soul. I'm always so impressed by her imagination. I don't know where she gets her artistic flare from.
"I'm grabbing a coffee. Would you like one?" Gill asked.

SOME PEOPLE AREN'T MEANT TO BE SAVED

"A coffee sounds perfect right now, thank you!"
I didn't even drink coffee usually but everyone's always ranting about its fueling properties and I definitely needed topping up.
These past few days have been so dramatic for reasons different to usual.
I sipped it... very, very slowly. It tasted bitter but I didn't want to be rude.
"I hope you don't mind me saying but... you appeared very tense upon leaving before. Would you agree? Please feel free to tell me to mind my business as well," said Gill.
"It was like I just realised I wasn't in the right place all of a sudden. When I was sitting there... listening to people share their stories, felt wrong. Like I was intruding. I didn't have a right to sit there pretending I had been through the same things they have."
It went silent.
I was questioning how she'd taken what I said. I wasn't saying anything bad.
"Can I ask, what made you attend today's session?"
"I uhm... well... I came because I thought it would help me make sense of everything I guess", I replied.
"And did it?"
"Well, I managed to reach the conclusion that I definitely wasn't being abused, so I think so" I said, confused.
I think the tone of my voice made her doubt my answer.
I mean, I'm not certain, but by the look on her face it sure seemed that way.
Maybe I was overthinking it.

SOME PEOPLE AREN'T MEANT TO BE SAVED

"If it makes you feel any better, it sounds like you came here with a really tough question. It doesn't sound like you were pretending to me. What I do think though is that you quite clearly have a lot on your mind and by the looks of it you're handling it by yourself too. I'm not judging by the way" Gill said softly.

It's strange how with one comment she was able to make me feel understood and less anxious but pressured at the same time.

"I've always wanted to be a 'strong woman'. Always. But I think I tried to be her so much for so long that people stopped worrying about me. Talking is something that I just struggle with no matter who it is. I don't know…" I said.

"I hear you. And I won't push you. But I'll leave you with this… If you have the opportunity to do something where the only risk is walking away with what you came with, then why not take it? Worst case scenario, it won't give you the answer you're looking for. But, at least you will walk away more knowledgeable than you arrived. Our groups… they're different from your generic state-run institutions. We care. I probably should not be saying that to you" - we both laughed a little.

It was nice to feel like subconsciously she understood my fears and restrictions.

As I've mentioned, my experience of the national health services here, is shameful.

I don't even blame the staff.

I used to until I realised who the real puppeteers were, orchestrating the act.

SOME PEOPLE AREN'T MEANT TO BE SAVED

No doubt, this won't be the last time I share my uncommon opinion with you.
Maybe it will help you understand me.
It might even help me understand more about myself. I need to connect the dots. Make sense of everything properly and maybe there are things I could learn from coming.
Maybe it could help me understand Ed's anger so I can stop it in its tracks before things really do get abusive.
Maybe this could be the answer I was looking for? One that meant I didn't have to leave him to clear his own shit up. Ellie deserves to have a dad growing up and if I'm the only one that has the ability to make sure of that, then I have to at least try right?
I wanted to say something back, but I didn't really know what to say.
As she took me to the room Ellie was in, I thanked her for taking the time to understand my situation even if it was just a little bit.
I really appreciate those small, exchanged moments. I never used to, but the more time passes, the more invisible I feel. So, to feel seen every now and then is such a unique feeling.
I walked to the doorway of the creche room and Ellie noticed me straight away.
She dropped her paintbrush and ran over to me with the biggest smile on her face.
I was actually smiling too - and crying a little. I gave her the biggest squeeze and swept her up in my arms.
I thought that ice cream at home would be nice for her.
We walked a majority of the way back home.

SOME PEOPLE AREN'T MEANT TO BE SAVED

We talked and laughed.
I couldn't believe how much she'd grown up and it was only going to continue.
She told me how much fun she had at the creche today.
It's amazing how much resilience kids have.
I feel like the world has been turned upside down and meanwhile, she has been able to adapt and grow – carefree.
The world works in peculiar ways.
I've spent most of this evening staring at Ellie.
Today could have turned out different but I'm thankful it happened. I know how that might sound.
What I mean is, if today hadn't of happened, I would probably have spent the night floating around in my own bubble.
Instead, I've spent every second of it with Ellie.
I hadn't checked my phone the entire evening, we watched film after film - until she bailed and conked out. And I really enjoyed it.
It's been a long time since I've been able to get lost in the blissful moments in life.
I didn't want those moments to develop into chores - something has to give.
I thought about calling Ed's Mum.
I know she wasn't the best but she's all he had and there was no point in calling his father. He's always breezed through life without a care for anyone.
It's no wonder Ed is the way he is.
I hoped I could change his view of the world the longer we were together, but the damage had already been done.

SOME PEOPLE AREN'T MEANT TO BE SAVED

I'm not quite too sure about how long Ed has actually been doing drugs.
I know that sounds bad.
It's something I should know right?
But every time I try to talk to him about it, he shrugs it off like I'm overreacting.
He really can't see the problem.
We met when he was 21 and I, 19. He was always on the party scene. I was young myself but even I didn't have a love for parties in the same way he did. It was like he craved them. He would sulk if he couldn't go out.
Sometimes he would rock in at 8am the next day. Sometimes he'd be out for days. No sleep. No shower. Minimal food. Just partying.
You've got to admit that's a lot, right?
I tried to talk to his Mum about it a couple of times and I remember how she'd laugh.
'That's just young boys for you', she'd say. She was never interested. It's like my concepts were alien to her. She was far too laid back.
If only she could see Ed now, I wonder if she would stand up then.
I always projected most of my feelings about Ed onto his upbringing. It might have been wrong for me to do so but monkey see, monkey do and all that.
The sooner people realise that their actions have consequences on real people the better. Because from where I'm standing, the world is pretty fucking broken and we're the only reason for that.

SOME PEOPLE AREN'T MEANT TO BE SAVED

I first found out Ed took drugs a few months into us being together.
I used to hear rumours, but he'd always deny them, and I didn't have any reason to not believe him.
But then I caught him.
He was coming out of the toilets with his mate. I tried not to assume anything, so I gave it sometime and stopped drinking.
I was used to people doing drugs, it's not so much that that made me feel uneasy. It's the lengths he went to, to hide it from me.
I should have known there was a problem then.
Turns out his Mum and Dad did more than just know about it. Ed's Dad used to fix their supply some weekends. It took me ages to find that out.
I understand that parents cannot control what bits of life their child decides to explore, but it's another thing paying for their fucking tickets there.
What's wrong in being the positive example that they're fucking obliged to be.
Sorry for my continuous swearing by the way. It's sort of a natural habit but I understand it's not for everyone.
These days everybody's a judge.
It felt weird not hearing from Ed today and to be honest, I wasn't sure if I was relieved or worried about it.
What if he's done something stupid? He never actually leaves me alone when I ask. It's been a thing for some time now.
Something didn't feel right.

SOME PEOPLE AREN'T MEANT TO BE SAVED

Instead of getting paranoid about it, I'm just going to have to go with the moment.
This time was doing wonders for my thinking process and I owed it to Ellie to show her how to hold her ground and be true to her gut.
I'm always critical of the messages I communicate to Ellie, without realising, but I'll admit it's been some time since I've done that.
The one thing I came away from today with, was that how I handled this situation would really impact her and I had to appreciate that.
On that note, I think I'm actually going to try and get some sleep.
I'll let you know how that goes...

SOME PEOPLE AREN'T MEANT TO BE SAVED

NASTY SURPRISES

Usually, I like to write in the order that my day has mapped out. But I really need to get this off my chest. I was so shaken up.
I was angry.
To be honest I was feeling a lot of shit feelings.
Things were just starting to feel quiet, but I should have known it would be too good to be true. Things never work out for people like me.
Why would they?
The world makes no room for people like me. We don't slip through the cracks; we get fucking pushed.
I try not to rant in here. I wanted it to be the one area of my life that actually made sense.
I tried to keep up with the paces of yesterday.
I started the day with no phone, I spent time with Ellie.

SOME PEOPLE AREN'T MEANT TO BE SAVED

I really fucking tried to put one-foot in front of the other, but I soon realised I was knee deep in quicksand - yet again! When I eventually turned my phone on late in the evening I had text, call and voicemail notifications on my phone.
In the pit of my stomach, I thought they would be Ed. I didn't think he would have been able to stick it out.
It turns out I was right but that's not who the missed notifications had been from.
Every single one of them were from Lee.
I couldn't even bring myself to check them.
One part of me didn't want to know what the big fuss was about, but then the me with responsibilities soon stumbled in and took charge.
Whatever it was obviously needed facing. I couldn't just keep ignoring things. It didn't stop me from thinking about it though.
Long story short, Ed turned up at Lisa's house.
Every fibre in my body was bricking it, in constant worry of what she was about to tell me next. Lisa was in a state when I called. Crying and everything.
Lee never cried and I'm not just saying that.
I've honestly never seen her cry.
I can imagine she would have cried when Mum passed of course, but I wasn't there to know.
My heart was racing, and my mouth went dry again.
I didn't know what to say.
She tried to compose herself, as she gave me a bollocking for not answering my phone.
I wanted to explain why I didn't answer but I just wanted to

let her have this moment.
Now wasn't the right time to start justifying things, she needed to be upset with me right about now. I tried to calm her down so that I could gain a clearer picture, but she kept hushing me.
I was starting to get scared now.
"What the actual fuck Alice?!"
She still sounded congested.
"I have been trying to ring you, text you, I've left you fucking voicemail after voicemail. Why is Ed showing up here? How does he even know where we live, Alice? I told you. I told you years ago. That man is not wired up right and now he's showing up at my door, Oliver's home Alice! Steve is fucking livid with me. He's been asking all sorts of questions and I don't know if I should be worried or not!"
She sounded so stressed out.
A tiny part of me wanted to ask her what she thought it was like to live with that same feeling day in and day out.
Why can't she realise that I didn't ask for this either?
I was just as scared as she was.
I was twice as unsure.
I live every day in fear of not being able to craft a lie that sounds real.
Of course, I didn't say anything though because then that would have hurt her feelings and I didn't want to do that. Is it so much to ask for the same in return though?
I get why she's angry.
If I had the luxury of the perfect homelife, I'd want to stay sheltered from all things bad and ugly too, but some of us

don't get a choice. And even when we are given one, the odds are stacked against us and we have to be willing to work ten times harder than the average Joe or Linda to have that better life.

"Lisa, I honestly had no idea that he would show up at your house. I'm so fucking sorry, I'm still in disbelief myself. Uhmm... Did he say why he was there?"

"Why do you think he was here? He was looking for you and Ellie. He's not just been once either, he's been twice. He's not long left and I am paranoid to shit Alice," said Lisa.

"Did he hurt you? Is Oliver, okay?"

"Well, the first time he came, it had just gone 8 in the morning. I told him you and Ellie were asleep because it was the first thing that came to my mind. He frowned like he didn't believe me. I honestly thought he didn't believe me, but he was so calm. He seemed fine Al, he said he'd try to catch on the phone and that was it!"

"Oh? I mean, it is weird that he showed up, but I honestly thought you were going to tell me something different!" I was so relieved.

"I haven't finished Alice…"

"Oh, you haven't?" I was so confused.

"He showed back up Alice. He came back this fucking evening. It was weird. It felt like he waited til Steve went and then just showed up! I can't actually be sure about that, but he was fine this morning" she started.

"And he wasn't fine this evening?"

"He was odd Al. He knocked literally a few minutes after Pete left for work. I saw him from the window, so I opened

the door. I wasn't sure what I was going to say but he'd seen me, so I had to answer. So, I answered. No 'Hi' or nothing. The first thing he asked was if he could come in. Obviously, I was thrown by that, I didn't really have a lot to say at the time and I wasn't going to say yes after the shit you've been telling me, so I said… no", said Lisa.
"You said no?"
"Hell yeah, I said no. What the fuck did you want me to say, he was on my doorstep Alice. I didn't have time to cook up some bullshit story…"
"So what? He just left?"
"No. He just walked in and I know he heard me. I heard me. He didn't make it past the second door but honestly, it freaked me out. He said you hadn't picked up his texts and that Ellie had an appointment tomorrow…."
I cut her off, "an appointment? What appointment?"
"I didn't ask, I honestly didn't have time Al, he wanted to speak to you and see Ellie. He got a bit agitated when I said he couldn't come in without me speaking to you first. After what you said, I was scared of what he would do. I had to tell him you weren't there Alice and I know you're going to be angry and honestly, I am so sorry, but Oliver was there. What was I supposed to do?"
I sighed.
I didn't know what to say at first.
I felt angry and sick.
That wasn't really her fault though, was it? I couldn't start ranting and raving at her. I would have done the exact same. It didn't stop me feeling angry though.

SOME PEOPLE AREN'T MEANT TO BE SAVED

"Al? Are you there?"
"Sorry, yeah. So where did you tell him I was?"
"I didn't. I wasn't about to drop you in it like that I just wanted him away from the house," said Lisa.
"Surely that made him angrier though? Did he react when you told him I wasn't there?"
"Now you come to mention it, I don't think he did, no. I must have been caught up in a moment of relief that I didn't stop to question his response actually. He was pretty calm. He still looked annoyed, but his voice lowered. He uhm… He said that I should have just told him and that he didn't want me dragged into whatever is going on between you two and that he's just stressed for obvious reasons and that he wanted to get a hold of you. I told him I'd get a message to you and have you call him. He apologised again and said he felt bad for showing up and being all crazy like that. Girl, if I didn't know anything, then I would have thought his fucking Oscar performance was real. He is good. But in all seriousness, I am sorry about flaking out and telling him you're not here" reasoned Lisa.
"Honestly… if I were you and things were reversed, I would probably want to do the same. In fact, I do it every day in some way shape or form. Panic and quick solutions have become almost like bad habits. Obviously, a part of me is like 'argh' and it just wants to scream but it's not your fault. I mean he still has no way of finding me. But he's already tried to tell you that I've abducted my daughter in an insane flit. You don't think he'd call the police, do you?"
"I think even if he did call the police and they got in contact

SOME PEOPLE AREN'T MEANT TO BE SAVED

with you and you explained the situation, I think they would see logic in your method. I wouldn't even worry about that. Listen, Ed is just going to have to deal with it okay. You've got this Alice - okay" encouraged Lisa.

"Yeah, you're right. Sorry, let me just check my phone for a second, stay on… okay so he told you he'd been trying to reach me or some shit, but I have no texts, no calls, no voicemails, nothing - how do you explain that? Also, I don't know what appointment he's on because Ellie hasn't got anything booked in. And the only thing I can think about is, have I actually gone crazy?"

"You haven't gone crazy okay; he's trying to make you feel crazy. I know we haven't spoken in a long time, but I know who you are Alice, and this isn't you. The reason you're here now is because you're putting Ellie first. If you say he hasn't tried to get in touch, he hasn't. Simple. Phones are shit yeah, but they don't fuck up that bad, it's obvious he's lying and trying to play games. You asked for space and he hasn't given you that. He's acting out to try and get your attention… he's a sly little bastard if you ask me" she ranted.

"Okay, okay. He's still Ellie's Dad. I need to respect that, there's got to be some way of gaining balance. If things go on like this, I'm not sure how much I'll take" I said hopelessly.

"This is what you absolutely don't have time for, and I know it's blunt to put it like that - I'm really not trying to put the pressure on or hurt your feelings okay, but you have to focus. I know it's not been much but from time to time over these last few days, I've really started to see more of the old you.

SOME PEOPLE AREN'T MEANT TO BE SAVED

You can't keep letting him destroy you because you think you can save him," said Lisa.
Tut "It's not like that!"
"Well, what is it like Alice, please explain it to me because from where I'm sitting, you're dying inside. I watched you move away and kept in touch. It was me that used to do all the travelling so we could see one another, never you. I watched you change into someone else. I watched you quieten down. I watched you disconnect from me in front of my very fucking eyes and now we're here. So please explain to me why you keep having his back, holding back how you feel and fucking justifying his actions to dance in the same fucking circles, he wants. You're my priority, Alice. You! When are you going to decide to be your own?"
Why don't I talk to myself like this?
I was feeling mixed emotions.
Part of me felt like I needed to hear that but another part of me still wanted to reject what she was saying.
I know how it sounds but it feels so wrong to speak badly of Ed.
What I say to him between us is one thing, but to actually bad mouth him to others. I felt like neither my head nor heart were programmed for that.
"I know you probably don't know what to say and I don't blame you. I'm not angry either, okay? I'm just upset. I want to protect you from this and just feeling like I can't be the shittest feeling I think I've ever had to experience. Mum would hate this; you know she would. Deep down you've got to know something's wrong babe. Do you?"

SOME PEOPLE AREN'T MEANT TO BE SAVED

"If we're going to have a conversation like this, we definitely need wine" I laughed.
I was sobbing a little too, but I don't think she could tell.
I think it was my way of lifting our spirits.
I was probably avoiding the question to be honest.
I'm starting to learn that I do that a lot now.
"Maybe that isn't such a bad idea. I know we've both got the kids, but Steve actually has the next few days off so…" hinted Lisa.
"So what? I've got Ellie, Lee. I can't just go off on a night out"
"I know that crazy. But… I could come to wherever you're staying. I could bring some food too, you're favourite…" teased Lisa.
"I don't know…" I said.
"Oh, come on Alice! It's been ages since we had a girls night in. I could come when Ellie's in bed and we can talk, laugh, cry, do what you want. You're bound to not be up for company at the minute and I would totally respect that if I thought that maybe I was a bad influence, but you need good energy around you at the minute. Someone who's going to keep you distracted. You know because I'm such a good laugh and that?"
I knew what she was trying to do.
Maybe I should just go with it?
I've quite clearly proven I can't stop or change things anyway so why not just learn to go with them?
And she was right about a few things she said tonight.
Either that or she just sounded confident saying them, either

way it was better than being on my own for another night. Who knows I might actually enjoy it?
Anyway, I agreed to it so long as she let me call her taxi and didn't tell anyone she was coming.
I've been off the phone for a while now.
I wanted to try and take in what had happened, but I just kept feeling angry and sick.
Then confused and upset.
Ed always calls me an 'emotional caution'.
I've reached the conclusion that I feel more than the ordinary person. I hurt and love extra than the average person. Or so it feels.
I feel like he uses it against me. Maybe he was trying to mess with me? He sure knows all my weak spots.
I've always been quite open with him.
Could I really put anything past him?
Anyway, I don't want to think about all that. It's late as it is, and everything always feels worse when it's late.
I don't know if that's a feeling everyone experiences, but I do. Regularly.
Though, as much as I hate the night, I also love it too. Strange, isn't it?
Aside from that, we'd honestly had a really great day, we even dropped by the centre again. I didn't make it into the room but, small steps, right? It was an excuse to get some more ice cream on the way back.
There was always tomorrow.
Speaking of tomorrow, I better get some shut eye.
I'm not tired but I always regret it in the morning. Ellie's

SOME PEOPLE AREN'T MEANT TO BE SAVED

been waking earlier than usual, and I honestly have wanted to cry most mornings.
I know it sounds selfish but I'm exhausted.
But I recognise that it's my own fault and, on that note, I am making the decision to have an early night.
Here's to making healthier decisions from here on out.
Fingers crossed.

SOME PEOPLE AREN'T MEANT TO BE SAVED

DRUNK THERAPY

I didn't wake up with the same motivation I had last night, but I wanted to try. That had to be a good thing, surely? Maybe a bit of progress?
Probably not knowing my luck.
I must be mad to think some time away was actually going to have a massive impact.
With each day that passes, I just know deep down that things are getting worse really.
I just wish I knew what to do to stay focused and objective.
It would be unfair to say I haven't made any progress flat out though wouldn't it?
I have, it was just minimal.
I know I was wrong to expect a quick fix. I just couldn't be arsed for the road ahead or finding out if things could even get any worse.
I think the pressure of the day was starting to dawn on me.

SOME PEOPLE AREN'T MEANT TO BE SAVED

Maybe that was why I was feeling so unsure.
I didn't think I could hack another day of unpacking my emotions. I haven't done anything physically and yet I feel so drained, it's crazy.
The days are the worst.
They just drag.
Some nights, I really appreciate the silence.
Most people are asleep and it's like it's okay for most of the world to just shut down for a bit and just be peaceful.
I wish the night dragged as much as the day did. It always feels like it's over quickly before it's the morning again.
I bet that doesn't even make sense to you. It made sense in my head.
Instead of hiding away, I pretended I wanted to keep up with yesterday's momentum, until it was too late.
We found ourselves outside the community centre.
Ellie ran straight in again.
I sort of wish she hadn't.
I was a bag of nerves.
Sometimes she just helps me feel more together. But I was happy that she was happy.
Of course, she ran through to the crafts class. I watched her go in and get stuck in.
Gill was heading out of our usual session room when she saw me standing in the reception area.
"Hope, you came. It's great to see your face. Will you be joining us?"
No matter how many times I was called by my new self-assigned name, it threw me every single time.

SOME PEOPLE AREN'T MEANT TO BE SAVED

My mind felt like a siv lately.
I was so consumed by the whispers of my own thoughts all the time that I stopped keeping up with day-to-day details. You've probably noticed that by now. I'm sure I don't need to keep affirming that.
It felt weird to be back in the same room, with the same people. I kept overthinking about what they must have all been thinking.
I felt like they kept looking at me. That could have been my paranoia though, so don't take my word for it.
Gill asked me if I'd like to speak.
As you'll probably have guessed by now, I was crapping myself. I didn't think I'd be put on the spot like this.
How weird is it going to look if I say no?
Obviously, I didn't say no.
Instead, I nodded awkwardly as I topped up on water and prepared to wing it.
"I'm just going to try and be honest. I'm no good at these things, I usually talk to myself as crazy as that sounds, so you'll have to... be patient with me at times"
I looked around the room, but no-one said anything. They didn't even move. Their faces were just sort of still.
I was even more anxious by this point.
"Okay. I'm Hope. Uhm... "
I looked at Gill and she smiled gently and encouraged me to take my time.
"I wasn't sure why I came at first and if I'm honest, I still don't know why I'm here now. I think I came looking for answers assuming it was just going to be that easy. This is

going to sound so bad, but I took my daughter and left our home 5 days ago now. You can think bad of me for that, I'd understand. I feel like a piece of... well I won't finish that sentence, but you get what I'm trying to say. I'm still not sure what it is I'm meant to be sharing or if I'm even in the right place!"
I went silent.
It stayed silent.
I wasn't sure how to feel.
Maybe they didn't think I had finished.
Was I finished?
"That didn't make sense did it? What I meant was, I came here because I was feeling isolated. I still feel lost. I'm not even sure if that's the right way to define it but it'll have to do. I'm trying this new thing out where I try to take myself out of my shoes and depersonalise the situation. When I think about the way my romantic relationship has progressed I realise I've felt less like me as time has passed. It's hard to actually even remember what I used to be like, before... well... before this. I feel empty. I doubt myself all the time. Am I doing enough? Could I do with making some positive personal changes? We can always be better right? I think I came here concerned for my relationship is what I'm trying to say. How do you know when yours is the abusive love story you've only ever talked about through other people's experiences? At what point do things become abusive? Because this shit is important to know if you're about to blow someone's life up and accuse them of abuse right? Well unless you're like me and have kids. Then things feel ten

times harder. All of a sudden it's not just me that gets affected by my choices. It's not just me soaking up the psychological repercussions. And then I think... What if one day it isn't just me that experiences the physical side of it. How long will it be before his behaviour pushes through the extra limits I keep setting every time I doubt his ability to surprise me. In fact, I spend most of my goddamn days asking myself 'what-if' questions and I'm just so tired right now. I feel so stuck. Like I know I should leave because things have turned sour. They've probably grown mould too because of how long we've left it, but it felt beyond repair. Though another side of me wonders about the impact it will have on our baby girl. She idolises her Dad. Give him his due, he was amazing at first. With her anyway. But that's all that mattered at the time. He tries now from time to time too. I just wish it weren't my responsibility to have to try and maintain that bond between her and her father. Is that selfish?"
Someone in the group actually spoke up.
"No. I don't think that's selfish" she said.
I looked at her and smiled. It meant a lot that she listened and took it upon herself to commentate on my thoughts.
I felt more at ease.
I won't go on too much about today's session.
I think I've got a lot more unpacking to do yet about that. But I left feeling much better than I left the other day.
It felt nice to go and be listened to by people who understand my situation - and some.
It's like I was more willing to take onboard their opinions

because they were actually talking from experience.
Maybe that's why I subconsciously ignore everyone else's advice.
They had no clue about what I was experiencing and that was okay, but it's okay for me to want my actions and thoughts to be understood too.
I need to learn how to communicate my feelings better to people or things are never going to get better.
Maybe in doing so, I could help other people understand and communicate their feelings better too. In a way that meant everyone was heard.
I don't know.
Sometimes I think I live in a dream land, but it makes perfect sense in my head.
I wish I knew how to express myself to people.
That really is the key to life. I don't care what anyone says.
Anyway, I had Lisa coming here today, remember?
What a whirlwind of emotions that gathering was!
She put me on the spot more than therapy today, but it ended up being worthwhile I guess.
We talked a lot of truths, shared a few laughs.
It was great. I cried during and after she left though, but I'll get to that.
You probably think I'm weird for wanting to ring her taxi, but Ed had already turned up at Lisa's, I just couldn't deal with any more surprises.
At the moment I just needed to make this journey as easy as possible for Ellie and I.
When she turned up, she was holding two bottles of

SOME PEOPLE AREN'T MEANT TO BE SAVED

Chardonnay.

I shook my head and laughed at her. I forgot how much she liked her wine.

"I'll still never understand why you always bring two bottles. We both know you're off this planet after half a bottle" I laughed.

"Like you'll survive one, I bet it's been a while since you've had a drink" she laughed.

The thing is she was right.

I felt a bit rubbish.

Only because I realised how much I had actually missed out on for a while.

It didn't affect my mood though; it was nice that we could have a laugh and so soon too.

I sat down without getting any glasses from the kitchen. I hadn't played host for a while.

Anyway, it wasn't long before Lee pointed out how thirsty she was.

She doesn't do things subtly. You'll probably have guessed that already.

That's what I loved about her though, you always know where you stand.

She isn't a people pleaser.

We were both brought up to have good intentions to be honest.

I assumed that most people were, but I was ignorant.

We're not all blessed with a positive upbringing, but neither of us are too good to experience the ugliest moments in life either.

SOME PEOPLE AREN'T MEANT TO BE SAVED

Mindfulness is something we were taught to practice in our group session today.
I was determined to try it out with Lee tonight.
I knew we were heading toward deep vibes. It was bound to happen with drink involved.
It's like your 'I don't give a fuck' filter switches off.
That's actually why I stopped drinking as much since being with Ed. I wasn't alert enough to guarantee that I could watch my mouth.
"Alice, can I ask you something?"
"If I say no, are you going to ask me again at a later date?"
"Probably"
We giggled.
"Then I guess it's important to you, so go ahead" I prompted.
She looked positively surprised.
I'm glad I made her feel understood.
It was a nice feeling.
"I've been thinking about how much I've loved how much we've spoken lately. It's made me realise actually how much I don't understand what's going on for you at the moment. So, the question I'm going to ask might be a lot for you, but someone needs to ask… what has been going on? Who the hell does this place belong to?"
"You like to get stuck in don't you?"
"You know me, bulls-eye kind of girl, sis!"
"What if your perspective is wrong though? I know how it sounds but just hear me out for a second…"
We had already had our first glass of wine.
My cheeks were starting to fluster, and I was feeling pretty

fucking honest.

I wasn't prepared for her question, of course not but the wine was helping.

I did mentally tell myself off every time there was a break in conversation. Overthinking about what she was thinking and if I should have missed bits out.

"When you think about it, how fixed are we as humans to be able to easily explain what is wrong with us? There's always such a pressure to know what's going on in your own life just because you live it…" I started.

"Carry on…" said Lisa in interest.

"Sometimes our problems escape a reality that words can't explain. I've been trying to pay more attention to how much attention I actually pay to my mental health as crazy as it sounds. Nothing has worked since I got diagnosed, but then again not much has changed either. Outsiders are always looking for a narrow version of the story. You just want to make sense of it so much that you're not too bothered about the daily log of events that led to today. I don't think I'll ever fully be able to explain what's wrong with me, I think that's going to take me a hell of a lot of time. I'm not even sure if I have the patience for it!"

I realised I didn't answer her about the bungalow, but she forgot anyway.

"Of course you do, why are you saying that for? Do you remember that time when I broke up with my first ever proper boyfriend? Mum hated him, remember? We were always arguing. Anyway, I don't know if you remembered but I had this habit of locking myself in the bathroom and crying. I thought no one would be able to hear but you told Mum about it. You both sat outside the door every day for two weeks straight. On day one, Mum said, 'Lee's baby, I know it hurts now and that nothing will make you feel better. I can't promise you you'll feel better tomorrow or for each day after that for a week even…' I sighed when she said that. I remember thinking what her point was if all she was going to do was remind me how much better I wasn't going to feel. Then she said, 'the best decisions are often the hardest to come to terms with, so it takes us a little longer to adjust to. You don't realise but you adjust slowly, a day at a time'. She said that you never feel okay after making difficult decisions but that you will always feel grounded as more time passes. Time is what you need now, Alice. What you need to decide is if this was going to be a permanent decision or a recurring one" said Lisa.

She triggered something in my thinking process.

I can't explain what, but it felt like she unlocked another area of thought I had yet to consider.

I had tried to avoid thinking about it but fuck it.

I might never get the chance to speak so freely again. And there was the issue.

"To you, there's only one question I have to ask myself. It's not that simple Lisa. Do you not think I've weighed out the risks of going back? I've thought about it and played out every possible scenario in my head. You think it's as easy as running away. Pfft, shit catches up with you. But I see your point of view too. If I go back, how many times am I going to run before I can't. Though there's all the messy bits as well like Ellie. I can't not let her have a relationship with her father growing up. I can't be that Mother and I don't want Ellie to be that child" I said confidently.

"Okay. So, what is he like as a Father now? Tell me a little about that so I can see some of the Ed that you see?" she asked.

"Well. He tries and that's what counts isn't it? We didn't have a Dad Lee. We did but you know yourself, he was always busy with his other kids. I hated that. It wasn't anyone's fault, but it didn't mean I wanted a Dad around any less"

I tried to get her to empathise with my thoughts.

"Yeah I get where you're coming from but if his efforts were enough you wouldn't have felt you necessarily had to remove both yourself and Ellie from the situation. Can you see where I'm coming from?"

"It does make a lot of sense and I suppose until now I hadn't really thought of it like that. Well, when you put it like that, I guess deep down of course I know the environment isn't exactly the best for her and of course, if I had to make a split decision to rehome Ellie, I'd pick the safer alternative every single time. I'm hurting yeah, and I've got a lot of shit to deal with right about now and she's probably watching more television than she should be but she's happy and safe and that's all that matters to me. Before I'm me, I'm a Mum. Every single time. I'm not saying she doesn't come first to Ed but if he could switch on me despite everything we share, then it was worth considering his other capabilities, too. I'm not a bad mother for making difficult decisions!"

SOME PEOPLE AREN'T MEANT TO BE SAVED

"So what's putting you off making the hardest yet?"
"Well for the exact reason you just stated… It is the hardest yet. I'm not just deciding to end a relationship. I'm putting a label on the nightmare that was the last four years of the relationship that could potentially end Ed's life. My decision could have the biggest impact on hers and her Fathers relationship and I would have done that. It doesn't matter if it was the best decision. How was I to know how she would internalise that as she got older. What if she asked questions the older she got or had to listen to rumours in school? For one second, try to take Ed and I out of the picture and imagine they're two other people in our situation. Ed's character, he has no one. His drug addiction has been enabled by people that were supposed to guide him as he grew up. He was always going to be tempted in an environment like that. Ed was Ellie, once upon a time. A child in a toxic home environment. Led by laid back role models. I think when we look at adults sometimes we forget they were once kids. I used to look at Mum and Aunty Joyce, Nanna and Grandad, any grown up really and I used to think they knew everything. I thought that once you grew up life was easier. I wished away my youth. Then I grew up and I realised that adults knew fuck all. It was laughable how much life felt like a game of survival. You had to battle real things like debt, finding a job, being able to eat, knowing who to trust, losing people you thought would stay forever, thinking about other people and then if that wasn't hard enough, you still had to make time to do what's right for you too. It's impossible. Someone's going to get hurt and what if

SOME PEOPLE AREN'T MEANT TO BE SAVED

I don't want to do that? I don't know, it's a lot to get into but what I'm trying to say is things aren't straight forward. It's like people have got used to giving up on others so easily. We're evolving to be selfish, inpatient little bastards and maybe I don't want to walk away from someone that needs help" I argued.

"I get that but where's the harm in thinking more into it instead of giving up on your cries for help too? You can't neglect yourself to tend to someone else. I get what you mean about the extremities of the way society has lost its sense of community spirit though. Why not compromise?"

"What do you mean?"

"Well, I agree, Ed clearly needs help and that bit you said before about Ed being Ellie once really hit home. You're right. It's hard to look at him and recognise that maybe he hasn't understood the way his childhood has influenced and impacted the person he is and that yeah of course he deserves that guidance like anyone else. But does that mean it has to be you that gives him that or do you want it to be you?"

"Of course part of me would love for it to be me but I know he sees past me these days. It's honestly like he's looking through me. My face used to calm him down, now it legit pisses him off, next level and then some. I don't think I could look at him the same even if I tried. It would be hard to forget all of this, and I think it would be hard to rewire my behaviour as long as he was around. I just feel like if I say out loud to someone else that I need to… leave, that I'll have to do it."

"I know you won't agree with me but maybe passing this

over to someone like the police could help? Maybe if you made it official you wouldn't have to worry about looking over your shoulder. That way you could go through the courts and a professional could help the two of you reach a decision in the best interests of Ellie?"

"You're asking me this like I haven't given it some thought" I said.

"No, I'm asking like I want to understand. Alice, shit is bad and those are only the bits you have told me. I can only imagine the shit you're keeping to yourself!"

"And would you blame me?"

"Of course not. I don't blame you for any of this!"

"You blame Ed don't you?"

"I mean yeah of course I do, and you can't expect me not to. Just like I can't expect you to right now. You were so right about how it came to this, there was no way he wasn't going to have picked up a few bad habits if his home life was so relaxed, I get that. But there's right and wrong, Alice, and Ed knew that every time he decided to do you and Ellie wrong, don't be fooled!"

"This is what I'm saying though. I'm not saying this situation isn't worthy of intervention, all I'm trying to do is consider the possibility that his concepts of right and wrong are different to ours and that maybe he isn't to blame for that. This is going to sound like such an odd way to describe how I feel but think of it like this… it's so easy to pass judgement on someone's life or situation and assume that that's what we would do if we ever found ourselves in similar situations. Truth is that life is so much more than dominant perceptions

of what's right and wrong. It's easy to be like 'Well why not just call the police'. I was always the first to shout at the television screen when watching similar stories on films, like 'CALL THE POLICE!'
Until I realised for myself that things were less straightforward than that. People can say what they like about what I have or haven't done and that's okay because I've sat on their side of the fence too. I can't expect people who haven't been in my situation to understand my vision, but it works both ways. Actually, being the one to decide that someone deserves to have their life ripped away from them… it's hard" I reasoned.
"I mean I don't agree but it doesn't mean what you're saying doesn't make sense. Whatever way you look at it though, he needs to learn that he can't get away with what he's done, Alice. He hasn't thought twice about the damage he caused to your life and neither of us understand yet the depths to which that harm will affect you in your life. He has to know that Alice, he can't be allowed to do the same to others he just can't. What if he gets into another relationship? Who's to blame then when he goes on destroying lives, having more kids without a care to how his actions affect the next generation?"
"I know what you're getting at and yeah you're right, I suppose that will have been down to me but I'm not suggesting that things be left. I just wish there were better alternatives, one that guaranteed him the help and support he needed. You probably think I'm crazy, but things are much messier in my head. I don't know where to start…"

SOME PEOPLE AREN'T MEANT TO BE SAVED

"Well as long as you know that I'm here for you every step of the way that's all that matters" said Lisa.
I couldn't help but smile. It felt like that was all I ever wanted to hear at that moment.
"You are being oddly nice. Who do I have to thank for that? You? Or the Chardonnay?" I joked.
"Cheeky bitch" laughed Lisa.
It was nice to move away from the subject, but I did feel better for the conversation.
It felt good to have my sister around, like old times. Laughing and sharing everything with no judgement.
"I've missed this. Laughing at the little moments. Catching up over a bottle. It's been nice so thank you" I said.
"You don't have to thank me. I'm sorry I didn't stick around. I didn't know things were this bad. If I'm being honest, I thought you were just happy to give up on everyone for him and that it was what you wanted. I didn't stop to think about the bigger picture. I feel so guilty for not being here while you've needed me but that's going to change, I promise."
"Don't feel bad for that, you're not a bloody psychic. You're a lot of things, but not that. I think if we're being completely honest, that's why I avoid opening to anyone close about things. I know no one else is to blame and as awful as it sounds, I don't have it in me to take this on and console everyone else. I know how straight to the point that sounds but I've always been able to be honest with you. No one could foresee how things were going to work out, not even me so please don't blame yourself. Even if you had recognised things were off, advised me and supported me, I

probably wouldn't have taken it onboard and I don't expect people to be patient with me while I suss things out for myself. Maybe things were just meant to be like this, they do say everything happens for a reason" I said.

"Or maybe, life's just shit. If you want me to be real with you, I think you've got to focus. This has happened for reasons before you were part of the equation, but this hasn't happened to you for a reason. But let me tell you that you will become part of the reason for anything that may or may not happen after that. Now you may not like it, but you've got to suck it up, and fast and ask yourself… what would you rather be responsible for?"

"What do you mean?"

"What I say. What would you rather be responsible for? Sending Ed to prison or for the harm that comes to the next woman?"

"Ouch!"

"Got to be said, Al. I'm just trying to be that rational voice in your head!"

"It's a good question, it's just… blunt. Can I think about it? Seriously. I'm not joking around. What you've said, although it's blunt, it's sort of right" I said.

I could probably go on for ages about the contents of the day, but the truth is there aren't enough pages to write on. All I can say is it's been a day full of thought. I don't think I've spoken as much as I did today for an awfully long time. I am a bit reluctant to share my story, though you will have probably grasped that I'm insecure in nature by now. It felt nice to let go and trust again today. I'm hoping so much that it doesn't get broken. I don't know how many times I can keep trying.

I'm a little nervous to go to the support group tomorrow but I think I've done well so far.

Baby steps, Alice. Baby steps.

SOME PEOPLE AREN'T MEANT TO BE SAVED

DIFFICULT TRUTHS

I've had so much on my mind and I still feel like there's tonnes left.

Although it was hard, I was starting to enjoy feeling like I was capable of piecing things together. Even if it was happening slowly.

Things aren't getting any easier, but it is getting easier to want to try.

I've been thinking about Pete a little, now things are starting to come together in my head.

It dawned on me in bed last night that while I've been spilling all of Ed's flaws to whoever will listen, that I hadn't even taken a moment to acknowledge my own.

For months, I'd been talking to another man behind his back. I know I wouldn't be happy if things were the other way round. Then again, a lot would be different if it was the other way around.

Some might say that they understand my reasons for

allowing myself to get emotionally connected to another man.
It was only written sentiments and with everything I had going on at home it's understandable that I'd need someone to talk to, right?
I know not everyone would be quick to defend my actions though, despite having a fuller picture of the years of turmoil I had just been subjected to.
There's a part of me that believes that too.
'If you're not happy, go'.
That's what they say isn't it?
A part of me would love to sit with these people for a moment and talk with them about their experiences in life. I'd love to ask them if they had ever experienced being afraid to leave a situation. For most of us it's the most natural thing in the world to be able to avoid the things in life that worry or annoy us, so much so that we assume it applies to any given situation.
I tend not to judge too much when it comes to other people's business, but I've learnt the hard way that not everybody is the same.
It's a shame we're all too busy judging everyone else's movements instead of minding our own business. I hope one day that changes.
It's been nice to listen to other people's perspectives a bit more.
When you're in my shoes, you get pretty used to the sound of your own voice echoing. Life isn't the easiest to make sense of at the best of times so to hear what other people thought was refreshing. It felt like a blessing.
Although I was feeling nervous about heading to the support

SOME PEOPLE AREN'T MEANT TO BE SAVED

group today, I was full of questions.
Not physical ones that I had planned out to ask the group.
More like key mental bullet points in my head.
Extra pieces to the puzzle.
Maybe another pair of eyes could help me piece my life together better than I ever stood a chance of.
If there's anything of value that I have taken from these last 9 days is that talking to other people does help. Not at first. I won't lie. But the more you talk about the same topic in different ways, the more vividly you are able to see things.
For all its truth and perspectives.
A problem is never just 'a' problem.
A problem is always more than what it appears at the surface.
Sometimes our problems come with roots.
I haven't figured out how deep mine go yet, but I'm sure as hell going to find out.
For whatever reason I don't get to watch Ellie grow up, I want her to know how to take care of herself, to know when to walk away and preserve herself and I had to start wanting that for myself if I wanted her to develop similar values.
It just feels so hard to want right now.
All this fucking time humans have been on this planet and we still don't have a guidebook on life?
Not even a life hack handbook, nothing?
Why fucking not?
How is that shit even explainable?
Why aren't we taught the real shit we need to know?
Like how to be an adult and survive parenthood while juggling other crazy shit.
Why does no one prepare you for how to deal with trauma if ever it did occur?

SOME PEOPLE AREN'T MEANT TO BE SAVED

They sound like pretty useful skills to me.
It makes no sense to only be given the opportunity to learn these things in therapy.
Looking after our wellbeing should be encouraged as a method of prevention before it is used as an intervention.
I think that's how I talked myself into giving the group another shot. It felt easier to talk and there with no pressure.
I spoke a bit about Lisa today at the group.
It has been nice to rekindle things with her since I've been away without worrying about what Ed might say about it.
"I can't believe how for such a long time I've avoided being the person I used to be to suit someone else. I was always compromising my own happiness for the sake of peace. Since I've been here I have been able to reconnect with my older sister and I can't put into words how I feel. It feels strange but has also reminded me of normality; something I hadn't felt for a long time. Lisa is quite a forward character; she says things that are necessary and really pushes me to reflect more from other perspectives. The thing is, she doesn't understand my logic for not wanting to involve the police and for the first time, I was forced to question my own logic last night" I shared.
"What thoughts arose when you were forced to question your own logic?" asked Gill.
"I can't say I'm sure... I feel... stuck? I guess. Her perspective made sense. But my perspective seemed to be blocking the reality of hers..." I don't know where that came from. It just rolled off my tongue.
Gill was nodding and staring at me empathically.
"What do you feel is keeping you stuck and blocking your sister's ideas?"

SOME PEOPLE AREN'T MEANT TO BE SAVED

"Today's reality of justice and ideas of what's right and wrong and how we go about 'punishing' them. This is a great group and I'd never want to degrade the work of some amazing professionals. Now, I don't know if everyone here feels the same way that I do but for what it's worth, the health services are neglected. No-one gets the help they really need and that stretches all the way from survivors to those with addictions, the homeless, the poor, offenders. When are things going to change? When are we going to open our eyes to the worsening damage to the things we can't see or measure reliably? Like mental health. No matter how many times people wanted to ignore the link between ill mental health and behaviour, the better. Mental health aren't symptoms of crazy syndrome, they're symptoms of trauma. They're symptoms of biological differences. We need to cater for this more in society. Who actually thinks that people like me - people like us - decide not to call the police because we're content with the idea of them being able to put others after, through the same? People like us, don't stand up because society has made it so hard to be innocent. Apply that to all sorts of scenarios, I am sure it will add depth to my concept. We don't stand up because it costs too much to be believed. We don't stand up because we've got so used to being kicked to the curb and then some. We don't stand up because we're being held down. But I'll tell you another reason why I won't stand up. I won't stand up because honestly, I don't think watching him get sent to prison will give me what I want. I don't even think I could get back what I wanted even if I tried and maybe I had to come to terms with that. It was a hard truth pill to swallow but I'm being honest. If I thrived off his misery, what would that make me?

SOME PEOPLE AREN'T MEANT TO BE SAVED

Equal? Or just as bad? Truth be told, I don't even think seeing him sent down would attain the change in him that he needed. If he was going to come out a changed man with a better interpretation of people and how to treat them, he needed the right guidance and support. If he was going to change for the best then he needed to be free from judgment when he was out, but our society makes that impossible. Things need to change. My sister understood that it was okay for me to want better for him. I realised I wouldn't be wanting true justice otherwise. I couldn't give her a proper answer to be honest when we were talking about it at the time, but I am super thankful she made me speak with her about it. She's helped me centre my focus a little better than I was managing to do on my own."
I couldn't believe I had got so much off my chest.
I didn't have a script in my pocket, it just rolled off my tongue the more Gill picked away at my brain.
That's how it felt anyway.
"I don't mean to sound sarcastic but that just gave me some fucking feels right there!" said one of the men in the group. He looked amazed.
"Oh really, uhm… thanks. I don't really like to share my thoughts with the world. I appreciate my vision is sort of different" I replied.
"That sounded extremely passionate, Hope, thank you for sharing your thoughts with the group. It sounds like you have been reflecting a lot in your personal time which is great. I don't like to sell people the self-awareness journey as one that's easy and… clean. The self-discovery path is messy. It's emotional. It's all about making sense of how you see the world, what you envision and how you want to live. It

SOME PEOPLE AREN'T MEANT TO BE SAVED

sounds like you've realised this without even recognising it and I just want to say that you are making positive achievements in your journey. I love the way you are willing to acknowledge the pressure that rests on the health care system. Most of us start with the enthusiasm to help others. But over time as funding continues to drop and staffing becomes more of an issue, that terrible sense of guilt kicks in because we don't need to be told we aren't doing our jobs. We know we aren't doing our jobs right. We start to resent our job because the odds are stacked against us and patients start to blame us, but we can't leave because then what? Who looks after my patients then? How far back on the waiting list will they fall too then? We feel all these things too, we experience burn-out syndrome and workplace depression, but we can't speak with you guys about it because it's ethically frowned upon. But where do people start to understand one another if we're always being forced to live by or listen to, one perception. I think what you said makes perfect sense, Hope. Does anybody have anything else they would like to feed into this discussion while it is still in motion?" asked Gill.

People started clapping.

It was such an odd moment but for the first time in a while, I felt like I belonged. Like I did make sense after all. I just haven't been talking to the right people.

I kept thinking about how nice it was that Gill immersed herself in my conversation and fed back her sense on what I offered.

I actually felt bad for all the times I blamed healthcare providers for their lax attitudes.

Maybe I hadn't been considering the pressures they might

SOME PEOPLE AREN'T MEANT TO BE SAVED

have been under.
We're all human.
We all have pressures and problems.
We're all slightly misguided, in different ways.
We all feel the same, hurt the same.
Feeling like they're letting people down all the time and the impact this takes on their mental health.
Remember when I was talking about roots and problems? Let's imagine health services to be the problem but politics to be the root.
Maybe we could start fixing things and building bridges. Teach people how to evaluate their problems, overcome differences.
Why does that have to sound so unrealistic?
It's not unachievable, we've just become lazy and hopeless.
We're the problem.
Power and people. And we're in denial about it.
I was glad that I showed up today.
I was starting to feel alive again. I felt like just mingling in with society was something I was learning how to do all over again, but I believed I could do it.
Maybe I did have the strength to live beyond Ed?
Maybe I was meant for other things and getting away didn't just have to be another dead-end what-if thought.
I feel like I'm trying to run before I can walk but it's better than standing still that's what I say.
Pete often used to remind me that our journey's only end when we die.
He used to say that ours too, like any other journey, will face halts, cross bridges and change course.
'It's life' he used to say.

SOME PEOPLE AREN'T MEANT TO BE SAVED

'What would you do if you were driving somewhere and then all of a sudden you just broke down. No petrol. Dead end! What would you do?' he used to ask.

I always used to try and joke with him in saying I'd call for breakdown assistance, but as usual, he always had a more punctual reason for the question.

If you're wondering what his answer was, don't worry I'll tell you. He used to say 'You'd walk. You'd get to your destination much later than you planned, but you'd get there. When we hit dead ends, when we run out fuel, the easiest option always seems to turn back. Yet, turning back always leaves us disappointed that we didn't manage to get where we were heading. There's always another way to get somewhere. There's always the footpath. Just because it'll take longer to get there, it doesn't mean we shouldn't set off. It's all about how soon you set off'.

'Maps, too,' he'd say, 'sure, they're handy to have. Directions make things easy. But again… you don't need a map to know where you're heading. You just need to know where you're going and stop fearing the travel'.

He used to say a lot of things that made sense actually, when you thought about it.

It's only been a short while I've been away from home, but it feels like it's been a lifetime. It's been slow and at times I wanted to head back too, but Pete was right.

I'd only be disappointed, turning back.

I wouldn't be going home to happiness. I wouldn't be going back to romance. I wouldn't be going back for love and I wouldn't be going back for me.

I'd be going back to shouting. I'd be going back to being to be the stress that caused him to continue – in his mind.

SOME PEOPLE AREN'T MEANT TO BE SAVED

I'd be going back to fear and I didn't want to feel that anymore.
I still don't escape the fear being here. He's in my thoughts when I'm awake and he's my nightmare when I'm asleep.
My dreams have been awful since I left.
Some of them are so bad, I wake up crying. It honestly takes me a while to calm down when I wake too. I have to sit in the bathroom some nights, just so I don't wake Ellie.
They were bad when I was at home but these one's are different.
Usually I can wake myself up when I'm dreaming about things I don't like but it's like he has a hold over me even when I'm sleeping.
In my dreams, it's like I'm motionless.
I can't move. I can't shout. I can't even talk.
And he's there. Every single time.
It's no wonder my mind is so exhausted. It's occupied twenty-four fucking hours of the day.
I just want a break from it all. I know knowing when to walk away is the only way out I have right now but it's so hard to stay self-managed at the moment.
I'm writing a little later than usual tonight. I think staying up late is my weird way of hoping it will prevent tomorrow coming any faster than it needs to. The days feels like they're passing quick, with bigger decisions weighting on my shoulders by the minute.
I just wished things would slow down a little. There's too much going on than I have time for. That's what it feels like anyway.
I don't want to keep being a negative bitch though. Today's thoughts had been useful for one thing – thanks to Pete.

SOME PEOPLE AREN'T MEANT TO BE SAVED

I needed to remember that I didn't have time to stop for breaks if I wanted to get where I was going any faster than I was. Ellie needs me to be strong right about now and I need me to be strong too.
Before I go I want to mark today as one that will remind me of where I'm heading.
No more stops.
No more breaks.

SOME PEOPLE AREN'T MEANT TO BE SAVED

KNOWING WHEN TO WALK AWAY

I was going to need a distraction after the day I've had. I feel like I'm always moaning but this is so hard.
One minute I feel like I'm charging in the right direction and the next I feel like I've forgotten the way there.
I needed to remember what it was like to feel like me again, and I knew I couldn't do that with Ed consuming my thoughts all the time and that meant being away from him.
I couldn't sleep last night while toying with the idea that maybe it was time to call it a day but the more I thought, the more I worried.
I hate change. But I fear Ed's reactions more.
I don't want to hurt anyone, but I can't lose myself either in the hopes that maybe he'll come back to me and that maybe things will be okay.

SOME PEOPLE AREN'T MEANT TO BE SAVED

I didn't want to break Ellie's heart, but it seemed the lesser of two pains.

I didn't want to give up on him but after all the damage done, I can't be the one to heal him now.

I'll never understand Ed and I deserved the right to heal too. There was no coming out of this untouched and Lisa was right when she said I had to come to terms with that. Everything I subject Ellie too will have an impact on her but what will determine her values is how she sees me handle my shit. It's okay for her to see Mummy make mistakes because that's life.

What matters is how I decide to show her she should handle that.

I didn't have to completely abandon Ed.

Maybe I could explain my idea to him about seeking support and getting back on track. Maybe he might see some sense in my madness and decide to go with it.

I know his Mum wasn't great, but maybe if she understood the situation for all the ugly it had grown to become, she would feel terrible. Maybe she had to see this too.

I couldn't keep shouldering the burden of Ed's secrets.

It was too much weight to carry between the pair of us, alone.

I know it would be hard at first, but things are hard now, right?

Difference is, with the way I'm going, things will only ever stay bad or get worse.

I started to feel confident about making that clean break but how was I going to break the news to Ed?

I think the most frightening part of it would be seeing how

SOME PEOPLE AREN'T MEANT TO BE SAVED

he would respond to the news.

A part of me thinks it would be a struggle to get him to cut ties.

I don't doubt he wouldn't make it as difficult as possible for me.

Anyway, I thought attending therapy today might help me figure out how better to approach the situation. I feel like when I share some of my thoughts with the group, I'm safe. I can be me.

I can express some of my deepest thoughts and feel understood and right now it wasn't just helping me. It was pulling me to shore.

A lady shared her story today with the group and she mentioned it had been the first time she actually felt ready to open up. I felt like she knew what she wanted to say, like she had figured something out.

I wanted to listen.

She explained about how up to now she's always felt like she couldn't trust anything she thought. She always doubted herself and it got that bad that she really couldn't handle making decisions by herself anymore. She shared that even right up until this week she felt like she couldn't be sure of anything that came to mind. It made me feel sad to listen to. She thanked me for sharing more about myself in sessions and how much it inspired her to start reflecting more on her own developing habits.

You don't understand how happy that made me feel.

To know that even though I was going through such a dark time, that I had still managed to influence someone.

SOME PEOPLE AREN'T MEANT TO BE SAVED

I felt like God was listening to my thoughts at breakfast this morning.
I felt like I needed a reminder about the person I used to be and like I got what I was looking for.
"I feel so humbled at the fact that I was able to help in some way. What a massive achievement by the way. I feel like this definitely deserves a round of applause, what does everybody else think?" I asked, looking around the room.
I was surprised that everyone joined in.
I felt like she deserved to celebrate her moment for the achievement that it was.
It's so hard to undo all the wrong that has been done to your mind when you feel like you've been stuck in a toxic limbo for a lifetime.
It's not undoable, but it is damn fucking hard.
It actually ended up being such a lovely moment.
"When all you're left with is your own thoughts, it's easy to go along with the idea that you might be crazy or stupid or any of those other nasty things we may be exposed to listening to in toxic situations. I remember pushing down my feelings or things that didn't sit right with me at times just to keep the peace. I think when you realise you've been living in the life of someone else, things start making more sense. You feel bad for questioning all those times you thought they had good intentions, because they loved you and you loved them, but they're valid questions that need valid answers. Not everything you think or say can be crazy? Unless that's what you're being made to believe. And why wouldn't you believe it? When you're being told something all the time, it

eventually sticks and from there… it breeds. Don't blame yourself, believe in yourself. I think that's what we all need to start doing a lot more. We need to focus on the distance we've travelled rather than the journey that awaits or the pace that we go at, for that matter. Every time I come here, you guys inspire me to think deeper and deeper. I came here with my own set of problems at first and not quite sure about whether listening to other people's experiences was going to make this process better or worse. I know how that might sound but I'm hoping you'll know my intentions weren't bad. You guys have helped me feel saner in a moment than my life has throughout its entirety."

I felt so emotional. It just came on in waves.

I forgot what it was like to feel teary in joyful moments.

Therapy was great today.

Ellie was getting on really well with all the other kids and I was able to freely explore my thoughts in a secure environment. Things felt like they made sense when I was there.

Oh, and when I was with Lisa of course.

Speaking of Lisa, I've been thinking a little more about her offer.

Being able to share a moment like that with the group today was amazing and it really got me thinking about some of my old friends.

I wish I felt like I could reach out to them, but it's been so long I don't even know what I'd say.

I decided to reactivate my social media account.

I hadn't been on there for a very long time and if anything, at least it meant that I could have a snoop.

It helped to get caught up in everybody else's reality sometimes.

Don't get me wrong it makes me feel shit about my life, but it also helped me to remember all the good that did exist in the world.

Being envious wasn't a bad thing, it was just another feeling.

It felt weird to login. I even forgot my password.

Ed always wanted to know what it was so when I was using it. He was always paranoid that I was moaning about him to the girls.

I think I'm now noticing a pattern about his uptight approach to me sharing details from our home life with others. Anyhow, I changed it before I deactivated my account in case he ever tried to access it without me knowing.

I remembered it eventually, to get to the point.

As soon as I logged on, I noticed I had a notification for a suggested friendship.

It was Ed?

He's never used social media before.

I wondered when the account had been set up, so I tried to find out, but his profile was under lock and key.

I checked his profile picture to see if there was a time stamp attached which revealed that he had at least had this account for a good year.

I spent ages wondering why he hid it from me.

It would be something he would expect me to mention to him.

I hate how it's always one rule for and another for another. I

bet he wouldn't see the big deal if I were to mention it to him though.
I started worrying after a little and decided to block his profile.
If he came up as a suggested friend on my account, I didn't want him to get the same notification and risk finding out I was on here.
I scrolled through, reading updates and looking at pictures. Everyone seemed so happy here.
People were getting married, announcing pregnancies, jobs and qualifications.
Things have been so different for me. Getting married wasn't what I pictured, it was a plaster.
Ed thought that after the beating he gave me when Mum died, it might make things better.
It was his way of proving that things were going to change. I wanted to believe him so badly that I did and now we're four years down the line and I can never make up my mind about the way I see things ending.
Either he was going to kill me, or I was going to end up killing myself one day.
I know I shouldn't dwell on things like that, but it helps me realise just how unhappy I am.
I knew today had to be the day.
I couldn't keep dragging things out the way they were heading.
None of us knew what was going on and we needed to move on with our lives.
Half of me wanted to use the social media profile as a lean

on excuse to end things because it felt easier, but I knew that wouldn't be right of me.

I just had to rip the plaster off and accept whatever was going to be.

I thought about ringing him, but I knew if I heard his voice, he would probably be able to win me over and that's not what I wanted, I'd made up my mind.

It seemed harsh to finalise things over a text though, but I didn't really have any other options.

I could write him a letter, but I just felt like I needed him to know right this minute before I had time to change my mind.

I picked my phone up and started drafting a message in my notes.

I was paranoid about accidentally pressing send before I'd finished the message.

The message I eventually drafted read, 'Ed. I hope you're okay and not frustrated by my text, but I thought it was time we spoke about what was going on. I wanted to call you but if I'm being honest I don't think I have the strength to row or dig each other out. There has to come a point where we realise that the fiasco going on here… it's toxic Ed. It's not that I don't love you anymore because I do, but things have wedged between us for a while now and I'm scared. I'm scared that you are getting beyond any means of control, it's like things are slowly starting to not matter to you anymore and I have to watch that every single day. We're destroying each other and we can't do the same to our little girl. She has to come first always. I don't want you to think I'm keeping you away from her either because I don't want that. Neither of you deserve not to be a part of one another's lives and I will never stand in the way. Right now, I think we need some time to work on ourselves as individuals before we can think about discussing anything else and I mean it. You need to take notice of the thing you stand to lose before it's too late, Ed. If I can't be the one to show you that anymore then I have to do what's best for me and try to get things back on track. I have enough to cover the rent that we're behind on to get things back up to date but after that you might have to think of staying with your Mum for a little while until you recover. I'm sorry I couldn't have done this in any other way, but I hope you'll understand. Al'.

I couldn't watch as I hit send. I don't think I would have pressed it if I did.

It had been less than a minute and he was already trying to call. I knew he wasn't going to take this lightly.

That curious side of me really wanted to answer but I knew it wasn't going to end well if I did.

I let it ring but he kept calling and calling until eventually I had like nine missed calls from him.

He sent me a text.

I don't even think I could physically bring myself to write down what he put.

He was saying all the things I had been wanting him to say for a long time.

A part of me wanted to fall straight into the trap and believe everything he was saying but I couldn't trust a word he said anymore.

His promises always fell through and I was tired of waiting

SOME PEOPLE AREN'T MEANT TO BE SAVED

on him to prove me wrong.
If he meant the things he was saying he would soon prove it.
We didn't have to be together for that to happen.
He was still always going to be a part of my life so it would catch up with me one way or the other.
All I wanted to do was what was best for Ellie and myself.
I couldn't keep letting him come between that.
I didn't reply to any of his messages, but it didn't seem to matter. His messages were nice until he started with the emotional blackmail.
The 'how he can't live without me' bullshit mantra.
He lived without me almost every other day on cloud flipping nine.
I was starting to feel disgusted by his complete wrong use of the word 'love'. He might have known what that meant one day, but now anymore.
It made it easier that I was starting to see him for all the flaws I was once happy to ignore. It made my decision easier.
I tried to block him out of my memory, but nothing was working, which is why I thought writing might help.
It's really helped break my nights down a little and give me a bit of structure.
Since I've been sitting here, I've had inundated texts from Ed as you can imagine.
Not only that, but Lisa has messaged too.
She said she was getting in touch to ask me if I had managed to arrange someone to go out with.
She said it was Pete's last two days off and that he would rather they watched Ellie tomorrow.

SOME PEOPLE AREN'T MEANT TO BE SAVED

It put me under a lot of pressure. I didn't even want to get in touch with any old faces.
In fact, it was the last thing I wanted.
She kept insisting it would do me some good.
She even offered to ring round for me but that just felt a little too much.
I get she was just trying to help but I don't want anyone asking questions.
If I was even going to go out, I just wanted to be able to forget about being Alice for once.
I wasn't going to be able to do it if I spent the night being interrogated.
Instead of sending all these texts out, I thought maybe I could test the waters by reaching out to one friend.
Their reaction would determine whether or not I was going to grow some balls and message the rest of the group.
It was taking a while to get a reply.
I almost thought I wasn't going to get one and when I did, I felt disappointed for getting my hopes up.
She said, 'Go on, what's happened with you and Ed?'
It sounded like she was waiting to cash out on a bet over my misery.
I just felt sick. It definitely put me off reaching out to any of the others.
Maybe I could just head out for one and then spend the night here making the most out of the peace.
I didn't have to drink, either. It's not like I particularly want to, I'd only be doing it to test Lisa's advice.
I couldn't tell Lisa I had anyone to go with, so I left that part

SOME PEOPLE AREN'T MEANT TO BE SAVED

out when I told her I was going to take advantage of her kind offer.

I was a bit worried about the fact Ed showed up the other day but now he knows we're not there, I guess he has no reason to show his face again, right?

I'll probably change my mind tomorrow or stick with it out of fear of telling Lisa about it.

It meant a lot that she had spent so much time trying to make things as pleasant as they could actually be at this point.

I didn't want her to feel like I didn't appreciate the advice and lengths she was willing to go to so that I could have some headspace.

I'm pretty exhausted now and if I plan to spend as much time with myself as absolutely necessary, then I am going to need to be clear headed.

I'll let you know it goes.

SOME PEOPLE AREN'T MEANT TO BE SAVED

A Harsh Reality

It's midnight. I don't usually write so late at night but I'm currently sitting here on my own feeling sorry for myself with a pizza.
I might be a little drunk too.
Probably not a good combination of events but if yesterday wasn't hard enough then I felt like God - if any - was trying to push me to every limit beyond the ordinary imagination. There really was no other reason to explain why things only seemed to feel worse when they should be getting better.
I remembered why I didn't like taking other people's advice again today and it just made me feel like curling up in a ball and staying there.
I went into the bedroom to spend a moment with Ellie.
I thought it would make me feel better, but I forgot she wasn't there.
I wanted nothing more than to lay with her. I've been feeling

SOME PEOPLE AREN'T MEANT TO BE SAVED

so overwhelmed with the responsibilities of being a mother while I've had the weight of the world on my shoulders that I've taken for granted how much better she actually makes me feel about my sad little life. I had the worst day today.
I should have never listened to Lisa.
I kept flitting from outbursts of tears to moments of silence and wide staring. I felt numb.
Maybe drinking at a time like this was only ever going to end one way.
I didn't even have anywhere to go but I still tried to push myself because I thought I was starting to feel ready.
How foolish was I?
'Go out,' she said.
'It's probably what you need,' she said.
Maybe what I needed was to start believing my fucking gut feelings instead of letting everybody else cloud my judgement.
To be honest I don't know what I need but I know shit is getting almost unbearable now.
How much more could I take? I'm only one person.
I didn't want to leave Ellie with Lisa today and especially not to go drinking.
I wasn't that bothered.
I hadn't been out for a while. I'm happy being a Mum and I lost all my friends a long time ago anyway.
They got sick of me 'needing Ed's approval for everything' or cancelling on the day. They often reached a lot of conclusions without speaking with me and whenever I tried to confide in them they never seemed to understand things

or even attempt to try.

To them it was just as black and white as it was to every other person that had never had to walk a day in the shoes of someone like me.

It was as simple as stay or leave for them.

It just ended up being one of those things.

I was sick of feeling pressured and they got sick of feeling ignored. I was reminded of that yesterday and instead of staying, I decided to go for a drink on my own.

I didn't tell Lisa. She still thought I was meeting up with friends, I didn't want her to worry.

She'd done enough of that since I landed back on her doorstep.

Part of me felt embarrassed too and I'd had enough of that for the last week or so.

Anyway, I thought it might be a nice opportunity to spend a majority of the night on my own after coming to terms with the shit storm that was my recent break-up, maybe I needed it, I thought.

But things didn't plan out like that.

Of course, they didn't.

I bet even you could have predicted that more shit was heading my way.

I didn't want to be anywhere too close to the bungalow so I thought I would head towards the support group and see if they had any nice places nearby.

I found a cute little bar about a stone's throw away so decided to head in there, with the intention of leaving after and taking a bottle of wine home.

SOME PEOPLE AREN'T MEANT TO BE SAVED

I walked up to the bar when someone tapped me on the shoulder.
I jumped out of my skin.
When I turned around, Gill was standing behind me.
"I didn't mean to scare you, love. I noticed you coming in and thought I'd say hello" she said.
"Sorry, I'm in a world of my own. I don't have Ellie tonight, so I thought I'd try something different, I'm only here for the one…" I said.
"Me too. One's about enough for me these days," said Gill. "Why don't you join me?"
"Yeah sure, thank you. I'll grab myself a drink and head over now. Can I get you anything?"
It felt nice being in a position to offer someone else a drink.
I was so used to not being able to do that, so to have a bit of money in my pocket that I didn't have to be worried about spending felt nice.
I'm thankful the conversation was a bit… normal.
I was worried she might have used the support group as a means of conversation, but things were so relaxed.
We both stayed for a second and I was already feeling tipsy by this point. I should have headed home when Gill did, but I didn't.
I stayed.
I think the alcohol was taking over and I started to just feel like I didn't give a fuck.
As I headed to the bar to get another glass of wine, I noticed a woman staring at me from across the bar.
I tried to avoid making eye contact, but every time I looked

back she was still staring.
I couldn't make out her face without staring and I didn't want to do that.
I started feeling paranoid so I reached into my bag for my phone so I could look distracted for a moment.
I was handed my drink as I noticed a message on my phone. My stomach dropped.
I told myself I would check it once I got sat down but I was distracted by what I could see in the corner of my eye.
It looked like the lady from the bar was heading towards me.
"Alice?" said a voice from beside me.
"Jade!" I wasn't expecting to see her face.
"I know what a long time it's been, do you mind if I sit with you? I'm waiting for a friend and it would be great to catch up" asked Jade.
"Yeah sure, sit down. You know, I saw you looking at me from across the bar and I didn't even realise it was you. How have you been?"
"I'm doing good actually. Me and Mike have tied the knot now. To be honest, I was trying to see if it was definitely you or not. I was thinking, no that's not Alice. Not all the way down here. How's Ed and little Ellie?"
I should have expected these questions. I didn't have any time to prepare my thoughts, so I said the first thing that sprung to my mind.
"So good. I'm away on work though so they're back home at the minute. Ellie's shot up; she's looking more like her Dad everyday" I lied.
"Aw, how sweet. I heard you and Ed got married. Elisha told

me. You two were meant to be together" she said sweetly. Oh, Elisha was Ed's sister. She's a bitch. Was never happy for me and Ed, she always liked to stir the pot. I know Jade wasn't still in contact with Elisha though, so I wasn't as worried.

"Yeah, it was amazing. Can't believe he still puts up with me, or me him either" I laughed.

Jade's attention was caught by someone walking into the venue.

"Jenny!" Jade shouted, waving her over.

My stomach dropped. I really hoped it wasn't the same Jenny I was thinking of, but it was. Ed's fucking ex! Jade didn't look like she was moving either, so it was quite obvious we were going to see one another.

"I don't know if you girls are going to find this awkward but maybe you could stay out with us, Alice?" asked Jade.

"We still have so much catching up to do. You don't mind, do you, Jen?" followed Jade.

"Fine by me," said Jenny. I could tell she was just as unhappy about it as I was. She was the ex that Ed really struggled to shake off. She was still trying to catch his attention a year into us being together. I mean it had been some time since, but I could still sense the tension. I definitely had to keep up with appearances now and make out like everything was okay.

"I'm going to get another drink, does anyone else want one?" I offered.

"Well I was thinking, since this has turned out to be a special occasion, how about I get us all some shots instead and Alice

you can fill us in on how your amazing little family are doing?" said Jade.
I really wasn't in the mood for either, but I felt like I couldn't really say no without it looking weird. It made it even more awkward that me and Jenny were left sitting together, I think maybe she did it on purpose so we could break the ice. We didn't. We fucking danced on it and sat quiet until Jade returned with the shots.
"Okay, so don't go mad but I thought I'd get us 12, so 4 each" said Jade as she was handing out the shots.
At this point I was feeling quite sober so maybe the shots weren't a bad idea after all. I needed all the Dutch courage I could get.
"How is Ed?" asked Jenny.
"He's... good yeah. He's settled down a lot now, not so much the party animal he used to be" I lied... again.
"Never thought I'd see the day. We had some good laughs when we used to go out. He swore he'd never grow up" said Jenny.
I think I mentally rolled my eyes at this point. She seemed to know him more than I did. Maybe I was stupid for thinking he'd ever settle down. We only got married in hopes that it would hold our relationship together. It wasn't.
"How time changes things, ay" I said before I downed another shot.
"You were always going to be the one to settle Ed down though, we all said it. He was besotted with you from the moment he laid eyes on you" said Jade.
Hearing that made me wonder if maybe I was doing the right

thing by leaving Ed.

It could have been the alcohol too, to be fair but either way I was feeling so shit about myself.

I let the conversation fall flat before saying I needed to go to the toilet.

I was anxious about leaving them and wondering what they'd be talking about while I was gone but being drunk helped me distract myself from thinking about it.

As I was walking back to our table from the toilet, I could see them whispering to one another.

I tried to walk slowly on the chance that I may have heard something, but Jenny turned around.

"Do you fancy going somewhere else? Jade and I were just thinking about heading to the club up the road. There's no music in here" asked Jenny.

It shocked me to be honest, but I thought I might as well.

It had to be better than sitting at home on my own worrying about Ed.

Jenny asked if I wanted to go to the bathroom with her before our taxi arrived.

I was a bit surprised, but I went with her anyway.

I was confused when she asked me to come in the cubicle with her, but I suppose girls are like that when they've had a drink.

She started rummaging through her bag and I thought that at first maybe she was on her period and looking for a tampon or something. Until she pulled out a bag of cocaine!

I was used to seeing the stuff though, so it didn't throw me that much until she offered me some.

SOME PEOPLE AREN'T MEANT TO BE SAVED

"Go on…" she said, "Help yourself!"
"Not for me thanks, I feel like I'm fucked just from those shots" I said, trying to play it cool.
"Oh come on… enjoy yourself. I don't believe for one second that Ed's misses don't do a bit of white every now and then" Jenny laughed, as she sniffed a key.
"What's that supposed to mean?"
"Don't get all personal about it, I'm just saying. I know Ed is a sucker for a good night and I thought being together you might be the same…" said Jenny.
"Actually they've never really been my scene if I'm being honest" I replied.
"What's your scene then? The library…" she laughed. "Don't be so boring, just try some".
I wish I wasn't drunk otherwise I wouldn't have caved into her pressure but all I kept thinking about was maybe it would try to help me understand Ed.
If I could understand what it was about that shit that kept him from committing to us, maybe I could help him after all.
It was a silly thought I know, but I took it.
As we left the toilets, I started to feel more alert and energised. I felt confident. I don't really know how to explain how I felt, but maybe it offered some reason as to why Ed had left me for the stuff.
It didn't last for long before I started panicking and feeling sick.
Jenny was making fun of me.
Jade managed to calm me down, but she was furious with Jenny for encouraging me to take drugs.

SOME PEOPLE AREN'T MEANT TO BE SAVED

She knew I wasn't a wild character - she was sort of similar.
When we got to the club it was loud and full of people.
It was nice to dance freely to the music and drown away my thoughts.
At one point I was standing staring at the ceiling and all the lights, just spinning.
My high had fizzled out after the first twenty-five minutes and I was starting to think about having more.
I'm not quite sure why, I honestly couldn't tell you.
A part of it made me feel close to Ed. I was struggling to get him off my mind.
I wanted to see him.
I thought about texting him when Jenny pulled me to one side and winked at me.
I knew what she was getting at, so I followed her to the toilets.
Jade came too, but she didn't look impressed.
I snorted more without even having to talk myself round.
I could hear Jade in the background but it's like I didn't care.
"I thought you said it wasn't going to be one of those nights. You do know Alice has never touched anything like this right? What do you think Ed's going to say if he catches up with her in that state and knows you're the one that got her like this because I won't be sticking up for you Jenny!" shouted Jade.
"Oh, shut the fuck up being so uptight will you. If Ed finds out and he isn't happy then that's his own problem. He'll probably thank me for injecting a little life into her. You don't think she'd have actually been any fun whatsoever if it

weren't for me fueling her up, for fucking free might I add. You're the one that told me to try… Here it is" she said.
"I told you to make an effort not get her fucking high" shouted Jade back to Jenny.
"Will you both just shut up? I'm not a fucking child. And Jenny, if you're so bothered about the money, help your bloody self, my bags there" I slurred.
The cheeky bitch actually started going through my bag as well.
I still haven't checked if she'd taken much.
I didn't bring a lot with me to be honest. I didn't expect to be making such a night of it.
"I tell you what, clearly you think I need babysitting…" I said to Jade, "And you, you were a jealous bitch then and a jealous bitch now. Don't think I don't know why you're keen to keep me out and shove your shit on me, you vindictive little cow" I said to Jenny.
"Jealous," Jenny laughed. "JEALOUS? Listen honey, I didn't have to force your hand. Acting like you're prim and proper because what? You think you're better than me? In fact, you think Ed settled with you because you were any better than me? It's fucking laughable. He settled with you because you were a safe bet. Someone he knew would cook his meals for him and hang onto every last thing he said and did because you're fucking boring, Alice. You were then and you are now. I feel sorry for you, Alice. Not envious" replied Jenny.
I slapped her.
I know what you're probably thinking but at the time it was

better than anything I had to say.
I forgot to mention that Jade had already walked out at this point. She never was one for drama and I'm sort of glad she wasn't there to witness me like that.
I half expected Jenny to smack me back, but she didn't. She was holding her face.
I could see my handprint start to raise on her face.
I really was trying to stoop to Ed's level tonight wasn't I.
"Maybe you have changed," Jenny said, throwing the rest of what was left in the bag at me.
She walked out and obviously, I wasn't going to follow her, so I gave it sometime in the bathroom.
I paced up and down with the bag in my hand.
I looked at myself in the mirror.
I even tried splashing my face with cold water but all I could think about was getting back out there.
Dancing and drinking.
Maybe I could find someone else to speak to.
Why waste the confidence trip I was on - that's how I was thinking?
I stared at the bag in my hand and thought about taking it, until eventually I did.
I didn't have any more, so I wasn't going to take anymore. I was just thinking 'fuck it'.
This hit didn't feel like the same as the first or the second.
I felt paranoid as I walked onto the dance floor.
There were a few guys outside the male bathroom as I came out.
They were laughing and looking at me.

SOME PEOPLE AREN'T MEANT TO BE SAVED

Well, that's how I felt at the time.
I just felt… uncomfortable.
My heart was beating out of my chest and all I could think about was a glass of water.
I can't remember if I fell on the way to the bar but that's what Johnny said.
Johnny was one of the guys I was telling you about hanging around the male toilets when I came out.
Anyway, one minute I was walking by myself and the next, I was being escorted to the bar.
It's bugging me that I can't remember certain parts but I'm hoping things might make sense after a bit of sleep.
Back to the story… I don't think I even got as far as to buy another drink.
I can remember Johnny whispering something into my ear and then us walking towards the toilets.
I know I was confused though. I can remember telling him I didn't need the toilet.
I even tried to tell him I needed to get back to my friend, but we were still heading towards the toilets.
I remember starting to panic as I saw we were heading into the male toilets.
I don't know how he got me in because I know I told him I wanted to head back.
Some of his friends were there. Smirking.
I tried to leave the bathroom but one of them stood in front of the door and tried to pull my top up.
I remember kicking one of them in his dick and spitting at one of them, in their face.

SOME PEOPLE AREN'T MEANT TO BE SAVED

I'd hoped it was hard enough to make him think twice about losing it before trying it again.
I ran into the cubicle and locked myself in.
I could hear people knocking on the main door to come in, but they soon went away.
I heard a few voices laughing and muttering.
It sounded like they were heading out.
I gave it a minute and then I unlocked my door and came out but before I could come out, Johnny barged his way through the door and locked us both in.
I was crying.
My heart was racing, and I just wanted to be at home.
For a second it felt like being with Ed was a safer option.
I closed my eyes as he tried to back me into a corner.
I kept feeling sicker and sicker.
I felt hot – something wasn't right.
And then I was sick.
All over myself. All over Johnny.
If I'm being honest with you, I wasn't at all embarrassed.
In fact, I had never been more thankful for something so embarrassing to happen.
He was absolutely outraged.
He pushed me to the floor, screaming at me.
He was covered in sick.
I could smell it.
It was a struggle, but I managed to get up and out of the toilets.
People were looking at me as I ran out.
There was sick all down my top and in my hair.

SOME PEOPLE AREN'T MEANT TO BE SAVED

I'm fairly sure it was on my trousers too.
I didn't think a taxi would pick me up in this state, but it did. I tried to act as sober as I possibly could, but I think I ended up talking him to death the entire way back.
I think I was just pleased to actually be on my way back than the alternative.
I know that maybe it would have been better if I had written tomorrow but I just needed to speak to someone.
There was no way I was going to ring Lisa at this time and in the state I'm in.
On the plus side, it might help me recall things tomorrow if I don't remember anything.
But, come to think of it, I don't think it would be a bad thing if I didn't remember any of this tomorrow.
I have made such a fool out of myself tonight. I can't even be sure if I've remembered everything.
I haven't even checked to see if Ellie has been okay either. None of this is okay.
I need to get a grip of myself.
What did I think I was doing?
I put myself in so much danger and anything could have happened. How was I any better than Ed?
I thought doing drugs was meant to be fucking fun.
I don't feel incredibly fun right now.
I better check my phone to see if I've had any messages from Lisa.
I forgot to check the text I got at the first bar.
I should have just left with Gill.
I've got a few messages and texts here, so I've taken a

SOME PEOPLE AREN'T MEANT TO BE SAVED

moment to brace myself before checking.
I can see Ed's name in the missed list and honestly the very sound of his name made me feel sick with anger.
The more I think about it, the angrier I'm getting.
I thought things couldn't get any worse after the night I had until I checked my phone to find out that Ed's got Ellie.
I've got to go.

SOME PEOPLE AREN'T MEANT TO BE SAVED

BEFORE IT'S TOO LATE

I'm sorry I left things so suddenly last night when I was writing. I had to get myself straight to Lisa's.
Luckily, she was still awake when I got there at like 3am. I still felt a little off balance given that I had only been home for 2 hours before rushing out but like hell was I going to let that bastard take my baby.

I knew he was a knob at the best of times but to be so fucking evil.

I did the same to him, yes. But he knows damn why I did despite liking to pretend he didn't.

I was filled with adrenaline; I couldn't stop shaking.

When I got there I was banging on the door and shouting Lisa's name.

A couple of the neighbours came on but if I'm being honest, I didn't give a shit.

Nothing else mattered apart from Ellie.

SOME PEOPLE AREN'T MEANT TO BE SAVED

I knew I shouldn't have gone out.
Anyway, Lisa answered the door. I didn't even wait for an invite. I just pushed past her on my way in.
"What the fuck do you mean Ed's taken Ellie, Lisa? How could you even think about letting him take her after everything I fucking told you?" I was stressed.
"Calm down, Alice..." Lisa said, crying.
"Calm down? CALM DOWN?! Lisa, you've just let Ed take my baby. Sorry, you've let him walk right in, take my baby and watch him leave with her and now I don't know where she is, and you think now's the time to be fucking calm Lisa"
"You weren't here Alice. He didn't really give Lisa a choice" said Steve in Ellies defense.
"Oh, and what the fuck were you doing Steve? Making sure you could do everything you could to keep the situation calm well let me ask you something Steve... If I had Oliver in my care and he had just gone missing like that, would you be just as calm then too? In fact, let me answer that for you because we both already know the answer to that. Now I'm going to ask one last time about what the fuck's happened to Ellie and I want one of you to start talking!"
"Steve, can you give us a moment?" Lisa asked while I sat down.
"You know I'm just scared, don't you, Lee?"
"Of course, I do, Alice. I am scared too, okay. Believe me if I could have stopped him, I would have done, okay. He planned this, Alice and he as good as said, it but worse" said Lisa.
"What do you mean, he planned it? That's insane" I said.

SOME PEOPLE AREN'T MEANT TO BE SAVED

"You've been saying to yourself how weird it's been that he hasn't been blowing your phone up as much as he was. That's because he's been watching my fucking house all the time. He watched you drop Ellie off today, he even said he was tempted to follow you back, but he knew by coming for Ellie that you would eventually follow. The things he was saying, Alice…"

"Okay you need to tell me everything from the beginning, and fast" I said.

"So we all sat in here and then the door went. I tried to look out of the window discreetly, but he saw me. Obviously, I pulled Steve to one side and let him know that for some reason Ed was standing outside our door. He couldn't believe it. I couldn't believe it. I tried to think as fast as I could, so I got Steve to take the kids upstairs. He was asking me all sorts of fucking questions and I just couldn't think. I told him I'd fill him in on things later and said that I'd get the door. So, I did. But he looked different. He tried to push past me into the hall, but I blocked his entry. He was asking to come in and take Ellie home so obviously I told him that I would get you and that he could speak with you about it, but he knew you weren't there. I had my back turned as he said it because I was in the middle of trying to wing my way to shutting the door on him. Honestly, Alice… It gave me chills. Of course, he knew it threw me because he was mocking the fact I didn't have anything to say. Of course, he was right, so I tried to say that I would get you to give him a call when you were back, but he started talking about how you were both over and that you had moved on with Pete? I was so confused. I told him he was talking nonsense and that I couldn't let him take Ellie, but he said the police were on the way. That's when he told me he had been watching the house. He told me that the police are under the impression that Ellie had been abducted and that you were mentally unstable. He said that because he was her Father that we had no right to withhold her from him. He said that he was taking Ellie whether I wanted him to or not and actually had grip of my fucking arm Alice. It's bruised. I shouted for Steve because I didn't know what else to do but the police showed up at this point and Ed had backed away from the door. I tried to reason with the police, but they said the dispute was between yourself and Ed only and that I was going to have to move aside. Alice, I broke down. He came about two hours after you dropped Ellie here, so about 8-ish. I'm so sorry Alice…" cried Lisa.

I didn't say anything at first and I could hear Lisa trying to get through to me in the background.

All I kept thinking was how long it had been since he had been to take Ellie.

Anything could have happened by now.

I wanted to believe he wouldn't do anything to Ellie, but I didn't think he had it in him to play spies and abduction.

"Why haven't you seen your phone by the way and why do you look as white as a sheet?"

"Do you honestly think now is a good time to get into all the finer details of this situation? I've got to do something; I can't sit here and talk…" I said.

"Alice, we have to call the police, you can't seriously be

thinking about dealing with this on your own? He didn't look like he was fucking about Alice and who the hell is this Pete guy? Has he got something to do with that nice bungalow you're staying in?"

"I don't have time for all of this, where are your keys?"

"For the car?" asked Lisa.

"Yes for the fucking car!"

"No, Alice. I can't let you. You've been drinking and you don't even know where they went. What good is going to come of it?"

"LISA!"

I know I was being awful and that deep down none of this was her fault, but I was so wrapped up in finding Ellie that nothing else mattered.

All I wanted to do was get out of that house and go and find my child.

"Here. If anyone asks, I don't know. You hear me, Alice?"

I hugged her and ran out of the door.

I could hear Steve ranting in the hallway about being irresponsible.

It didn't faze me though because funnily enough, this was the most responsible I felt for a long time.

What else was I supposed to do?

I'm not taking his shit anymore.

I'm not dancing to his fucking selfish little tune.

Living in silence because I'm too scared that things will explode.

Maybe that's the only place it was heading to begin with.

How blind was I.

SOME PEOPLE AREN'T MEANT TO BE SAVED

How stupid was I.
I thought by getting away and being somewhere he didn't know that he wouldn't be able to get to me.
But he knows how weak I would have felt without him.
Of course, he did.
And, now that I think about it, it makes sense that he hadn't pestered me as much as I expected him to because he was still able to slither into my mind from a distance.
He knew I would have caved and reached out to Lisa.
He knew how much we loved each other before he destroyed that too - and now he wants to destroy me.
I felt like I had given up trying to understand him for the last time. He knows how much I dote on Ellie.
He knows I'll do anything to protect her too.
So, if it's me he wants, then I'll give him what he wants. I'm not running anymore.
The only thing I could do was head home and take things from there. He didn't really have any other options that I knew of, so it seemed like a good idea.
I couldn't stop thinking about the night I had just had and that angered me even more. I was putting my foot down so much I hadn't realised I was speeding. I just couldn't control it.
I don't mind the way that Ed wants to treat me.
I'm not saying I can handle it, but I'm a big girl.
But to use our daughter in some sick realm of manipulation to get to me sickened me to the pit of my stomach.
I tried not to think about what was to come.
I wanted to stay at the height I was at for a little while longer.

SOME PEOPLE AREN'T MEANT TO BE SAVED

Enough to be able to face him for the last time to let him know that this is the last time he gets to take the piss out of me.

I didn't understand why I wanted so desperately to get away when Pete offered me the opportunity that he did.

I was so confused.

I felt like I was acting out of the ordinary. But at this very moment, everything made sense.

He had never taken away the person I really was, I just hadn't been her for a while. All I had to do was spend some time with myself for a while to begin realising that and that's what threatened him.

When I pulled up the lights were off at the front of the house. Maybe they were in bed? I thought.

Anyway, I got to the front door and realised I didn't have my key. I was so annoyed. I didn't want to knock, and he knew that I was here.

I wanted him to be just as unprepared as I was for a change. I was fed up with always trying to do the right thing when up to now it had literally gotten me nowhere.

We always kept a spare key under the wheelie bin, but when I went to check, it had gone.

I was honestly starting to freak at this point.

I hadn't made it to this point for nothing.

I didn't want to start losing my head, so I had a check to see if maybe he'd moved it and low and behold I found it. It was at the side of the house under one of the plant pots.

I did have a moment of hesitation before I put the key in the door.

SOME PEOPLE AREN'T MEANT TO BE SAVED

I didn't know what was coming and it just freaked me out. Anyway, when I got in it was silent. I tried to tip-toe up the stairs because ours were so creaky.
It felt so strange to be back at the house. Stranger than arriving at Pete's for the first time.
I poked my head through Ellie's door first. It was too dark; I couldn't really make out if she were in her bed or not. I wouldn't have put it past Ed to have had her in with him for the night.
He probably expected me to come the same night.
"Ellie..." I whispered.
I couldn't hear anything, so I switched her light on.
She wasn't there.
I had to stand for a moment to take in a deep breath.
The only other place she could have been is in our room. I crept across the landing and opened our door, but they weren't there!
My heart dropped, and I broke down.
They couldn't have been downstairs and to be honest I was running out of hope so I didn't even want to kid myself believing they might have been.
I ran downstairs and into the kitchen, hoping I might be able to find something that would give me some idea on what to do next when I saw an empty envelope on the dining table. On the reverse was Pete's handwriting - addressed to me of course.
It made sense all of a sudden when I remembered that Lisa had mentioned Pete before back at the house. I hadn't actually thought about the practicality of him finding out.

SOME PEOPLE AREN'T MEANT TO BE SAVED

He must have been going through my things.
I was so confused though because I didn't just leave them lying about.
I used to sneak them out with me on the way to take Ellie to school and throw them in a bin on the way.
No particular bin, just any I could find at the time.
If he has found out about Pete and that's why he's taken Ellie, then what else does he have planned? I don't know why, but something in the back of my mind kept telling me to check if the passports had been taken.
I took the drawers to pieces in the kitchen but couldn't find them.
I ran upstairs to check if anything had been taken to find that most of their clothes had been taken and the suitcases had been taken from the wardrobe.
I raced downstairs for no reason.
I didn't know why I was charging down the stairs like I had a plan because I felt so out of options.
They could have been anywhere by now.
I felt so weak but there had to be something else I was missing.
Sometimes we used to leave each other notes on the fridge. Nothing sweet. Just errands or tasks. I checked to find that he had left a note. It didn't give me anything to work with. It said, 'Alice, I have taken Ellie for a 3-day holiday. I know it's last minute, but I thought you'd want to be in your own home for a bit. Back soon.'
I was so confused.
He hadn't mentioned anything about Pete.

SOME PEOPLE AREN'T MEANT TO BE SAVED

Nothing about everything that's been going on and it sounds like he's trying to be normal.
Oh, he's fucking good.
Showing up with the police, feeding them a load of shit.
Now he looks like the good guy for taking Ellie away and giving me some space in my house.
Also, I'd like to know where on earth he seems to have found this money to take her on holiday. Something more had to be going on, but I honestly just felt too powerless to start unpicking it.
I felt like every time I took a step, the world took three and all of a sudden, the obstacle course that is my life became harder to accomplish.
I'd already wasted so much time so that's why I decided to sit down and think but it all became too much. I had a million and one different thoughts racing around my mind and I couldn't seem to silence them. I couldn't drown them out.
I tried to cover my ears. I even tried techniques I'd learnt through CBT but what a fat load of good they were.
I still don't even know how that was supposed to help. How was learning to manage my thoughts and behaviours any good if I didn't understand why I was doing it?
More to the point, jack shit was working, okay.
I know it sounds crazy but that's why I decided to start writing everything down.
I know it sounds surreal but writing everything down has really helped me to reflect on things so much.
I have learnt to pick up on things I need to improve.
If I hadn't, I probably would have ended up back at home the

SOME PEOPLE AREN'T MEANT TO BE SAVED

very first day. It's helped me recenter and think better.
It's helped me realise how much Lisa has supported me from start to end with this.
It's helped me to realise, that I can fucking do this.
Okay, Alice. Think.
If I call the police now and they show up here and all I have to give to them is some goddamn friendly note, they're going to laugh me into the crazy home that Ed is working overtime to get me into.
It made me wonder if maybe he had known about Pete for longer than recently, but I don't have the time to think about that now.
If I take a moment to look at things logically, Ed doesn't have anywhere to go. I highly doubt he even has any money. He could have got his hands on some so I shouldn't be dismissive of that but the chances of it seemed unlikely to me.
I can't afford to take any chances here so the most logical thing to do would be to follow the one lead I have. The only thing I could think of was to call Lisa.
"Lee, I haven't got much time, okay so don't try to talk me out of anything. I'm at home but they're not here. They're clothes aren't here, and neither are their passports. Ed's left a note like everything's normal. It's short and explains he will be back in a few days, but we have no money or anything. I'm going to the Airport, okay and when I get there, I'll be sending Ellie in a taxi to you. Okay?"
"No, Alice. None of this is okay, you're putting too much pressure on me and I really think we should call the police

SOME PEOPLE AREN'T MEANT TO BE SAVED

now?"
"Okay…" I said.
"I'm serio… Oh? Really?"
"Yes, Lisa. Ring them. I'm going to need some back up. I just hope it doesn't backfire in my face" I said.
"Whatever happens, you know I'm here and you know I've got you, yeah?"
"Uhm… Okay, I've got to go. Keep an eye out for Ellie and send me a text when you've spoken to the police. I'll check it as soon as I get the chance" I said.
"I love you, Alice," said Lisa.
"I love you too, Lisa. Goodbye"
I still wasn't sure if my plan was even going to check out or if I even had a hope of finding them, but I couldn't stop going. I worried if I did, that this would be it for me.

I'm going to need some money so maybe passing by the bungalow would be a good idea because I'm not going home until I know where Ellie is.

Once I've got there I'll head to the airport and wish for the best.

I'm just hoping I don't lose my bottle by then.

SOME PEOPLE AREN'T MEANT TO BE SAVED

THE END OF THE ROAD

I had to pull over on the way to the bungalow. I almost crashed. I just wasn't thinking straight. How many times did I feel like I was going to stare hell in the face before life started to get that little bit easier?

I really wanted to believe that I had a plan, but I didn't.

I felt stupid, weak and powerless.

Do you know how hard it is to carry on even when you feel like it's time to stop?

I don't want to stop but I'm tired.

I was driving around with little sleep, no food and to top it off I was on a comedown.

My mind kept flitting from the evening I had to the situation I was in now.

All I had to focus on was making sure my baby girl was safe and sound and back where she belonged. I couldn't keep subjecting her to this drama and as much as I wanted Ed to

get the help he needed, he continues to back me into a corner. I don't even think I'm strong enough for this. Never mind relaying a four-year timeline to officers that forget about it the minute they leave work. I could go through all of this to be made to look crazy and dishonest.
Argh!
So many things were going around my head, but I knew I had to keep going.
As I was driving, I kept thinking about letting the wheel go or spinning the car out.
I felt like I was going to fall asleep at the wheel.
I had never been exposed to such a series of events before.
Is it any wonder I was feeling the way I was.
I arrived at Pete's, eventually.
It was 5am now and the neighbourhood was quiet.
I had to go back to the car because I realised, I'd left the key inside.
I must have forgotten to turn the lights off before I left because most of them were on.
I was sure I had turned them off, but I was in that much of a rush, I couldn't be sure.
I headed straight to the bedroom and noticed the curtain blowing at the window.
I definitely knew I hadn't left any open as that was something, I was always paranoid about.
Curiosity was getting the better of me, so I decided to check the window.
As I did, I felt someone pull me down to the ground by hair.
It was Ed.

SOME PEOPLE AREN'T MEANT TO BE SAVED

I was begging him to let go but he wasn't having any of it.
I tried to ask about Ellie, but he wouldn't answer me.
He dragged me through to the kitchen and threw me across the floor and into the cupboard.
I felt stiff, like I had no control over my body.
I was frozen.
"What the fuck have you done to Ellie, Ed?"
"Same old Alice. Always more bothered about something else. You haven't even asked me how I got here, how I knew you were here. That was the part I was most excited to talk about. I take it you don't feel the same then?"
He sounded cold as he spoke.
I hadn't seen him like that before, I'm sure.
"So, what, you want us to do the same old bullshit we do? Dance to your tunes, play your fucking games. I'm tired of its Ed and I'm tired of you. I know exactly how you found me do you really think I'm as stupid as you have me believe? You really thought little old me couldn't piece things together all by myself. No of course you didn't. You never actually thought I was incapable of figuring things out, you've just been scared of not knowing when I might actually stumble on the fact that you're a manipulative little bastard and that's why you're so angry now, isn't it?"
He knew I was taunting him, but he still couldn't stop himself from biting.
He picked the closest thing up that he could, stood up and threw it at me.
I thought about dodging it, but he would have only got more pissed off if he'd have missed.

SOME PEOPLE AREN'T MEANT TO BE SAVED

I couldn't imagine how things could possibly get any worse and from how things were playing out, I didn't have much else to lose.

"That's it, you do what Ed does because instead of listening, this always works better right? It usually shuts me up… but not this time Ed, now I'm going to ask you one last time, where's Ellie?!"

"You never did know when to shut your mouth did you…" snarled Ed, "maybe you need reminding".

I screamed as he dragged me from the kitchen to the bathroom.

He was pulling me towards the toilet.

He lifted the lid and put my head down it as he flushed it. I could hear him laughing, to him this was honestly hilarious.

I could feel myself panicking, trying to grip a hold of the toilet to maybe push myself up but I had no control over my body.

Maybe this was it. I thought this was it - I was actually going to die, drowning in someone else's toilet.

All I could think about was Ellie and how I let things get to this.

He pulled my head out of the toilet and went to wash his hands.

I was feeling weak, and my eyesight was impaired.

I could smell the toilet water in my nose.

I tried to slither across the floor. I thought if I could get to the bath that I may be able to pull myself up, but he turned round as I was moving.

He stood there laughing at me, taunting me, telling me he

wasn't going to tell me where Ellie was and that I'd never find out either.

He told me it was all my fault and do you know what, I believed him.

He was right.

I know I should have kept my mouth shut but I wasn't just going to give up easily.

I scanned the room to see if there was anything, I could use to defend myself but the only thing I could think of was the toilet brush and I didn't imagine that to be the most effective tool but it's the only thing I could think to use.

I thought maybe if I could get into the kitchen, I'd have more to work with but then so would he.

I was pinching myself.

I was trying to draw myself back into the moment.

I knew there wasn't a chance I was hallucinating, and I needed to think fast.

"So, when did you plan on telling me about this sweet little setup then? I'm taking it that this is what you mean when you said you were sorting things?" asked Ed sarcastically.

"I know you know Ed so cut the bullshit" I said.

He grabbed me by my throat and dragged me up.

I tried to say something, but he gripped my neck tighter.

My head started to feel full, and my airways were blocked. I couldn't even manage to breathe through my nose.

I wasn't about to go down without a fight.

I pinched underneath the arm he was using to hold me up until he dropped me.

He tried to grab me, but I managed to run out of the

bathroom.

I didn't have time to shut the door behind me, I just kept running until I got to the kitchen.

I ran to the drawer and thought about picking a knife up, but I didn't want to kill him for god-sake. I just wanted to stun him, so I had time to get out of the house.

I saw my bag on the counter and went to reach my phone as he came in.

I was starting to think that I wasn't going to come out of this alive, I felt like giving up.

"Give me your phone Alice..." Ed demanded.

He held his hand out, expecting me to put it in his palm but I unlocked it instead. I knew I was pushing boundaries, but all exits seemed to be closing in on me.

I didn't have any other options.

"Give me the fucking phone, Alice" Ed said while rushing to the kitchen drawer.

He pulled a knife out and held it up towards me.

"Or you can always do what you need to, and I'll just have to follow suit" he said, raising his eyebrows.

I felt numb.

I dropped the phone and watched his face light up and he lowered the knife.

"Good girl. I don't want to hurt you. I'm hurting, Alice. I love you and Ellie so much. It cut me up to read your secret little love letter. Running to other men for the attention you need and spouting your lies off, for what? For a place to live. We've been together 8 years, Alice. Does none of that mean anything to you?"

SOME PEOPLE AREN'T MEANT TO BE SAVED

I knew I should have been trying to talk him down.
It would have been the better option, but I was going out of my mind trying to imagine all sorts of scenarios or things he had done to Ellie.
"Help me understand you Ed, seriously. Because you have to admit that things just didn't get like this because of nothing. We lost you a long time ago because you're so selfish. You never take a minute to stop and think about how your actions have consequences for me, for Ellie. You have the nerve to make me feel bad about Pete, like I've done you wrong? Please. I've never met the guy; I haven't slept with him or anything like that, but shit get lonely when you realise that something else, always has to come before me. I sit in that house day in, day out. I'm a shell of the person I used to be. You blame me for everything that goes wrong in your life, hit out when you can't get your fix and I've had enough, Ed. I'm sick of walking on eggshells and trying to be the nice bitch that always finishes last. I'm sick of being calm just so I don't tip you over the edge and I'm fucking sick of not knowing where your edge actually ends. I tried to understand you tonight. I thought that if I could figure out what was so good about that shit, I might actually be able to help you, but you're a lost cause, Ed. Do you hear me? Lost, fucking, cause"
He looked angrier with each word that rolled of my tongue. He ran at me with the knife in his hand, so I dashed round the breakfast island to try and avoid him.
I was so close to the door, if I could just get out, maybe someone would try to help.

SOME PEOPLE AREN'T MEANT TO BE SAVED

I picked a plate up from the side and ran.
He caught up with me, but someone was at the door.
He dragged me away from the window.
"Keep your fucking mouth shut" Ed whispered slowly. "I should have known that she knew you were here the whole time. How could I have been so fucking stupid! Well, if you think she's going to make a difference about what happens from here on out, you'll be fucking disappointed"
I thought about screaming but he was digging the knife into my lower stomach.
One word and I don't doubt he would have shoved it right in.
Tears were rolling down my cheek.
I sat there as Ed wiped them off my cheek and told me to grow up.
"ALICE!"
It was Lisa.
Part of me was thankful but the other part of me wanted her to leave.
She'd been through enough; she didn't deserve this as well.
"I know you're in…" she shouted through the letter box.
"Any smart ideas of how to get rid of her?"
"She's not just going to go away, Ed," I said.
" Well you better think quickly then otherwise I'm going to drag her in here too and you can die together" said Ed.
The world just felt like it was closing in on me and there was nothing I could do to stop it.
I thought about suggesting opening the door.
Maybe we could both make a run for it in time.

SOME PEOPLE AREN'T MEANT TO BE SAVED

There was no way he was going to run out in broad daylight on the streets with a knife.

He was many things, but he wasn't daft enough to get caught. Maybe I shouldn't have banked on that.

I told him the only way she was going to go away was if she heard my voice for herself, but he told me that it wouldn't work.

I had cuts on my face, my hair was still drenched from the bathroom and my clothes were torn.

I told him that maybe I could shout it through the door. I could just tell her I wanted to be left alone right now until the Police had something to come back with.

He thought the idea was the best we had to work with and let me head towards the door.

"If you even think about trying to run, you'll regret it, do you hear me?" said Ed. He looked serious.

"Don't I always fucking cover for you. What makes you think this time will be any different?"

"Don't try to play games, Alice. I mean it. Be quick!"

I walked into the hallway.

I could see Lisa's shadow through the door.

For a moment I felt safe, but I knew that was about to change.

"Lee, are you there?" I shouted.

"Yeah babe, it's me. I haven't heard from you, I thought you'd be at the airport by now. Let me in!"

"I... I can't right now Lisa. My head is all over the place. I went to the airport, but it was a dead end. Looks like it was just another one of Ed's fucking games. I called the police and they said it would be best giving them any leads we may or may not have and staying somewhere he couldn't get to, so I came back here…" I said, trying to sound as convincing as possible.

"What's changed? I mean it's great to hear you've decided to leave it with the police but why the change? Call me crazy for even thinking this but I couldn't shake the thought that he was here?"

She lifted the letterbox slowly.

The small part of me that actually wanted to survive, was hoping by some sort of miracle, she'd see me and help me.

But the rest of me was sort of hoping that she wouldn't.

As she lifted it, I saw her eyes look at me and widen.

It must have been in shock - I did look pretty rough.

But then I heard Ed walk up behind me and realised her eyes were looking past me.

She screamed.

I ran.

I kept thinking about running up the stairs until I realised, they weren't any.

Wherever I went, there was no escaping him. He was going to get me.

I hid beside a bookcase in the backroom, hoping I'd blend in. I could hear him smashing things.

"If you don't fucking face me, right now, Alice… I'll just have to have some fun with Lisa. I'm sure she's dying to come in and see what all the fuss is about…" Ed said.

I thought he was joking but I could still hear him taunting me as he walked to the door.

I couldn't let anyone else get hurt because of me.

SOME PEOPLE AREN'T MEANT TO BE SAVED

I saw the key dangling in the door to the back garden. Maybe I could distract him somehow and save myself at the same time.

My idea seemed silly at the time, but I went for it.

I peered out from beside the bookcase and started turning the key.

As I managed to open it, I threw a book from the case into the front room to catch his attention.

I could hear him trying to find where the noise was coming from.

As I stepped into the garden, I saw him in the front room. I was trying to lock the door, but I was panicking and dropped the keys.

I could see the knife in his hand and by now he was already wound up. There was only one place that knife was going, and I didn't want to take any risks.

I tried to inhale some deeper breaths as I picked the keys up and locked the door in a hurry.

I didn't have time to take them out, so I left them in the door. The fences were a little high but if I could get into the garden next door, maybe they might be able to help.

I still wasn't sure whether or not Lisa was still round the front.

I didn't know what to do.

I tried to climb the fence, but I kept losing my grip.

I could hear him trying to throw books at the door, presumably hoping he could smash the glass.

I wanted to scream for help, but I didn't want to anger him anymore than I had to.

SOME PEOPLE AREN'T MEANT TO BE SAVED

I managed to get up the fence but as I did something came through the glass.
I managed to swing my leg over the fence, but he grabbed my other.
I screamed as I fell from the fence onto the floor.
I banged my head as I fell and when I opened my eyes, he was standing above me.
"All that and it's still going to end the way it was supposed to. Did you really think I was going to let you go so easily? I've tried to be a better man for you and your demanding expectations. I've done my best too to keep up with this bullshit, picture perfect family life you'd always dreamed about in your goddamn, stupid head. But you always wanted more didn't you. Did you ever stop to think about why it was so easy to fall into addiction, living with a suffocating, boring little bitch like you" he laughed.
I was weak but not weak enough to have the final say.
"You fell into addiction because you're a weak fucking bastard, Ed. Always have been and you always will be. And if you think for one second that when you kill me all of that is going to go away, you're wrong. I tried to help you, Ed but you never wanted to help yourself. No. Instead it served your purpose to keep up with fake pretences, blame me for everything and still get away with putting yourself first without feeling like it was fucking unreasonable. You took everything from me, everything. Fuck knows what you did to Ellie and now you're just going to what? Kill me because you can't have everything you want? Because things aren't going your fucking way. Well, I tell you what, kill me. Kill

me right now if it will make you feel better"
"You really like to make out that I'm the bad guy don't you. I haven't killed Ellie you stupid bitch. But she is far away from you and when I've finished here, all she'll know is that you chose to leave us. You won't even be a happy memory to look back on. You'll just be the cheating bitch that didn't want us anymore and you know I'll make her believe it, so I hope all of this was worth it" he smiled.
"ARGHHH!"
Smash
Ed was led on the floor as Lisa stood above him.
She was shaking.
"Is he dead?" asked Lisa, scared.
"I can't feel a pulse" I panicked.
We could hear sirens outside.
I didn't know what to do. Ed was just laid there on the floor.
"Alice, the police are outside. What do you want to do?" asked Lisa.
I could hear that she was speaking to me in the background but it's like I floated off somewhere else.
I stared at Ed's body on the floor hoping he'd move but he just didn't.
How did it come to this? How were things alright one minute than like this the next.
If Lisa hadn't shown up, I would have been dead, but I didn't think for one second it was going to be a him or me situation.
"Let them in," I said.
I noticed Ed's phone laying on the floor beside him.
I wasn't waiting for the police to believe me again. Not if

there was a chance, I could find Ellie.
While Lisa let the police in, I put his phone in my pocket.
I stood there taking everything in as the police surrounded Ed and closed off sections of Pete's house.
Of course, they started asking questions, but I just wasn't ready to talk. Lisa managed to sway them to question me later before she took me outside for some air.
We went to stand outside when I saw an ambulance pulling up. I felt sick.
"What did you hit him with?" I asked Lisa.
"Uhm… I think it was a plate. I didn't know what else to use. I tried to find something that wouldn't cause too much harm but... I'm so sorry, Alice but he was standing over you and I just reacted…"
"If anyone asks. it was me, got it?" I spoke.
"No, Al. They'll understand it was self-defense. I left you all those years ago but I'm not going anywhere now, okay?"
"I'm not asking you Lisa" I said.
All the neighbours were outside. Well… most of them were. I couldn't bring myself to look at any of them, I knew they were just here to be nosy.
I felt so ashamed for disrupting Pete's reputation, he was so well known here and from what I imagine, he probably never involved himself in trouble.
They all looked shocked.
If they weren't ushering their kids away from the door, they were covering their mouths, or holding their cheeks in utter disbelief.
I thought to check Ed's phone but was worried the police

might have recognised it was missing.
I couldn't stand around and wait to be questioned or for Lisa to open her mouth.
This ended now.
I wasn't letting anyone else get hurt.
I walked over to the officer that looked the most approachable and asked if I could have a word.
I told her as much as I could at that moment, but I'm sure I'd missed details.
Everything was still a mess in my own head, I needed to make sense of it all first before properly explaining it to anyone else.
All I kept thinking about was needing to know where my baby girl was.
I don't believe in God, but I found myself praying to him a lot. I kept hoping that Ed was telling the truth and that she was alive and well.
I felt sick.
As expected, they took his phone from me and asked me to come down to the station with them for proper questioning.
They made Lisa come too.
I didn't want to go with them.
I put up a bit of an emotional fight.
They didn't seem to have much patience with me. To them, they came here with an objective and wanted to see it through.
I just wanted someone to understand the emotional turmoil I was going through.
It felt like my heart broke into thousands of little pieces. I

SOME PEOPLE AREN'T MEANT TO BE SAVED

wasn't in the mood to sit in a police station and be questions. But I guess it had to be done.

SOME PEOPLE AREN'T MEANT TO BE SAVED

LIFE AFTER

It's been months since I've written anything, I'm sorry. Things have changed in the short time I've neglected putting pen to paper.
I can't believe we're down to the last few pages.
You're probably wondering what I'm up to now.
I've just had so much going on, I've tried to avoid revisiting things in my head and here too.
I just wanted to forget everything.
Ellie's home where she belongs after thinking I'd lost them both.
Ed had taken her to his Mum's house.
The police brought her home to me the same day after they checked Ed's phone.
You can imagine just how overjoyed I was to have her back in my arms.

SOME PEOPLE AREN'T MEANT TO BE SAVED

Nothing else mattered.
Oh, and we hadn't killed Ed by the way, which I was of course grateful for. I don't think I could have lived with myself if he had died.
He's not here though.
He'd been arrested.
He was refused bail as he was considered to be too much of a risk.
We still haven't had the trial yet.
I think that's what's more annoying. I thought that once he had been charged, things would start sorting themselves out.
I came to learn though those things weren't going to feel any easier for a long while yet.
I was naive to believe that leaving would have been enough.
In fact, I was naive to believe that there were any easy exits, at all.
For me, getting over this was going to be harder than it would have been to stay.
I wasn't sure I was capable of starting a whole new life again, but I knew it was the only way things were going to start getting better.
I knew it was going to take time and I'm thankful I stuck things out because I'm just starting to believe that there might be more joy to life.
I'm not saying that healing banks on time and time only, because it relies on so much more than that, but it helps.
Not at first.
Never at first.
But with each week that passes, I've learnt to adapt.

SOME PEOPLE AREN'T MEANT TO BE SAVED

Don't get me wrong, there wasn't a day that Ed didn't intrude on my thoughts as he trespassed through my mind.
I worried about him all the time.
I hadn't been able to speak to him since he tried to kill me and I'm not sure if that made things better or worse.
I felt like I had so many questions I wanted to ask him.
I wondered if maybe he had things to say to me too.
I stared at the ceiling most nights wondering how he'd be feeling or if he was asking himself the same questions I was or even if he felt guilty.
Surely being clean for all this time, he was bound to be in a more rational state, right?
It was rare I opened up to anyone about the situation for all the excessive thoughts I had, apart from when I was with the support group.
I'm still going by the way.
In fact, things have really changed since I last wrote.
I'm not quite sure how, and I still can't believe it myself some days, but I'd been asked to take on a voluntary position with the team.
I co-led group sessions, with Gill, twice a week and I honestly loved it. It was nice to feel admired for my experiences for a change, instead of being avoided because of them.
You'll be pleased to hear that they finally know me for my real name now.
Although it felt strange to hear them refer to me as Alice, I was finally starting to feel free again.
We left Pete's bungalow.

SOME PEOPLE AREN'T MEANT TO BE SAVED

It didn't feel right staying after I had trapsed all that trouble to his door and I don't think I could have coped with the embarrassment of facing the neighbours after.

We came back to our home for the meantime, at least until I knew what was happening with Ed.

It was weird to be there, but Ellie was so happy to be home and it meant that Ed had somewhere to send Ellie letters.

I know no-one understands why I'm still trying to be the bigger person but it's important I stayed that way, both for myself and him too. I didn't want him to feel like him being in there was my sick sort of way of seeking revenge.

I didn't want him in their full stop but there was little I could do. There was no convincing society that prison wasn't the answer.

The way I make sense of it, the only thing I'd be walking away with is an empty verdict from people who knew nothing about him, nothing about me and nothing about our situation.

A bunch of people rummaging through our business with no appreciation for any emotional baggage attached.

Ed, getting sent down risked him coming out worse than he went in.

Forever slapped with a label on his head.

You tell me… Who would want to change for that?

Who would want to change knowing that they would only struggle to live an ordinary life anyway?

Who would want to change, knowing that most people had already made up their mind anyway?

It doesn't sound very rehabilitating, does it?

SOME PEOPLE AREN'T MEANT TO BE SAVED

The type of justice I wanted was more than a custodial sentence could offer.

I wanted this to be the reason he decided to change, not get worse. Otherwise, what would be the point?

I shared this with the group a couple of weeks ago and do you know what? They loved it.

I mean I went on more of a tangent that I have to you, but it helps you catch my drift.

They obviously admitted they hadn't thought to question the modern society before in the same way I had but that wasn't what mattered.

What mattered was being able to get a group of people to hear my perspective and make sense of it without thinking I was still under some sort of spell.

I'm not a long-distance victim.

I just think that he deserves the chance to heal and repair in the same way that I do.

If not, I'd be an enabler and I wasn't about to let him suck my good intentions out of me, no matter how much he tried. I'm stronger than that.

Lisa still believed that Ed wasn't meant to be saved and that there were things that people had to do on their own. She thinks some people just aren't ready to confront their problems as quickly as others and maybe she had a point.

I can see why it would make sense for people to think like that, but I didn't agree.

We don't learn how to help ourselves; we are taught how to help ourselves.

I've spent months, dragging my arse through what felt like

SOME PEOPLE AREN'T MEANT TO BE SAVED

hedges and hills and bushes and trees.
I didn't make it here because I was ready to address the root problem in my life.
I made it here because I was given an opportunity. Opportunities don't come around for all of us though and certainly not for the guilty.
Pete used to say it was everybody's responsibility to ensure a safe environment and that we all played our part in some way to jeopardise that or influence that.
I always told him that there was a fine line between the two. We used to talk for ages about our views on the world and what we'd imagined it would be like if maybe we all just cared a little more and made decisions that were based on rights rather than ease.
If we really did treat everyone else in the way that we'd expect to be treated. If we led rather than managed. If we empathised more than we depersonalised.
It sounds all tinsel and sparkle, but anything has to be better than the life we live now.
The thing is no one wants to fight for what is right anymore because no one wants to listen.
Bad shit happens and that's just that, as far as most are concerned.
You learn to live with it and move on.
But what could happen if we chose to learn from it instead?
What potential could that have for victims and survivors?
What potential could it have reducing behaviours that we had come to put up with?
They say you can't avoid bad things happening in the world.

SOME PEOPLE AREN'T MEANT TO BE SAVED

I say, bullshit.
Let me say it louder for the people in the back.
Bad exists because of trauma. It exists because of difference and ignorance.
And let me tell you where I know it manifests… It manifests in the actions and behaviours of mankind and it continues to filter down generations.
We will never get rid of the bad in this world until we understand why it exists, but I don't see everyone uniting to realise that anytime soon.
I want better for Ellie.
I want better for her children.
I want better for everyone.
So maybe, just maybe, you might be able to see me less as a victim who's still held down by the damage inflicted. Maybe you could learn that it's okay to heal without hatred and malice being the driving force of that process.
I understand things a lot better now, but it doesn't mean it hurts any less.
It just means I'm one step closer to being able to kick trauma's butt and start understanding on how best to help others.
You can probably tell how fitting this new role was to my personality. As much as this experience has been awful, it's also taught me a lot of things that really, I think we should have grown up learning and understanding.
Instead, we're stuck in a vicious cycle of bad shit because no one wants to get their hands dirty and really understand the trauma process and its knock-on effects.

SOME PEOPLE AREN'T MEANT TO BE SAVED

Let's just say, I've learnt to think more before making rash decisions.

Some criticise me for my tendencies to overthink but I'd learnt that for all its downfalls, overthinking had positive impacts too.

I wouldn't have got this far winging it.

You're probably wondering where all this has come from, especially since I haven't written in a while.

I'd be lying if I said that there wasn't one final thing playing on my mind.

Ed has written to me from prison.

I've had the letter for a few days now. It took me a day to build the courage up to read it.

I knew where it was from as soon as I saw the envelope.

No one else knows this yet. It hasn't been something I've exactly wanted to share with people. I knew it would come with so many questions that right now I didn't have the answer to.

He told me that Jenny was stepping in to offer him a character reference.

Jenny was the ex of Ed's I was out with when I wrote to you a while back.

It annoyed me a little to find out it was her that had offered to rise to the challenge.

Of course, it did. I wouldn't be human if it didn't.

I didn't want to begrudge him for his support just because it pushed my nose out of joint.

It made me feel better to know he was being supported but a part of me wondered why his Mum hadn't stepped in to do

SOME PEOPLE AREN'T MEANT TO BE SAVED

it.

He hoped Ellie was well and asked about how she had been getting on at school.

My heart dropped when I read that he had asked to see me. It's been playing on my mind ever since.

Not because I'm thinking about going but because I couldn't figure out why he would want to see me.

I had some ideas but all of them sat wrong with me.

I wish him the best for both his and Ellie's sake, but seeing him...? I don't think I was ready for that. Not even after a few months.

As much as I feel like I've learnt how to start feeling more like me again, I definitely didn't feel strong enough to see his face.

I don't just want to disregard it, but I think it's best I don't toy with the idea now.

That's why I thought I'd write it down, that way I'd feel like I'd spoken to someone then.

It's sad I won't ever get the chance to tell Pete how grateful I was for the kindness that he showed me in a time I most needed it.

He'll always be at the centre of my survival story.

I used to be ashamed of our connection and his part in my story, until I learned that he was the best part about it.

He helped so much to restore my faith in humanity, in ways I hadn't realised up to now.

I've learnt not to look at my old friends with resentment for abandoning me.

Instead, I learnt to understand that no-one was free from

SOME PEOPLE AREN'T MEANT TO BE SAVED

trauma in situations like these. I shouldn't have expected my friends to burden this abusive situation for as long as I wanted it to continue because in doing that, I would have been asking them to go against what they thought was right. I understand why they couldn't stomach it sticking around. The things I shared with them must have been emotionally damaging and I'm glad that they chose to avoid that.
Maybe one day they could begin to understand why I stayed. Why I had to go off and do me when I did. Why I had to figure this shithell out for myself.
I'm so glad that I did.
I'm so glad that for the first time in a long time, I chose to do what was best and not what was easy.
A few of them have actually been in touch but all their messages sort of communicated the same thing. I could sense they felt guilty, but I wasn't ready to console them just yet. I needed to console myself.
I felt awful at first for ignoring their messages but then I realised it was okay to heal at my pace.
As soon as I'm feeling a little more capable, I'll reassure them then.
None of this was their fault and they had no guilt to shoulder.
I don't know what to relay to you with regards to Ed's letter. Maybe I could suggest a call, instead?
What he had to say was important in how things played out next for his recovery.
All I know is right about now, I can't look him in the eye. I could handle listening to his voice, maybe but looking at him while I had to do so? I think that would be something I would

struggle with.

I'm not saying we're still going to be constants in one another's lives. I'm just saying that the very least we owe, is to close the book properly.

I didn't want Ellie growing up with animosity towards her father.

I didn't want her growing up with trauma that she didn't understand or know how to deal with.

It made sense to take the opportunity to show her how to be the best person she possibly could, no matter what anybody else did.

To always be a good influence and to never get consumed by the bad.

Someone once told me that whatever you weren't changing, you were choosing.

I have come to realise the sense of this in so many ways, lately.

I choose happiness.

My story is scattered.

There is no order to it.

But it's the truth. For all the ugly, the bad, the overthinking, and the negative thoughts.

This has been me for a long time.

It was nice to get the chance to know the me that was. It's helping me change into the me I am today and for that, I will always be thankful for.

I'll let you make of it what you will…

Writing this all down in a notebook for a man that will never see it seems silly, but you really have kept me going in my darkest moments.

I couldn't make sense of why you sent me this book, but I guess it was just another one of your hidden lessons that I was bound to learn more about sooner or later.

No doubt I'll write again as I stumble through the next chapter of my journey as I continue to learn more about who the hell I'm supposed to be after this.

But for now, rest well my love.

SOME PEOPLE AREN'T MEANT TO BE SAVED

AUTHOR BIO

Summer Kaur is a Ba Criminology and Criminal Justice student, mental health campaigner and author of the new novel, Some People Aren't Meant to be Saved. With a passion for writing from a young age, Summer has developed a real creative pleasure for connecting people with books. Her work is popular for the way it allows readers to rummage through reality and make sense of the world – speaking to readers from all backgrounds.

Printed in Great Britain
by Amazon